Planning and Control of Sports Training

Planning and Control of Sports Training

T.K. Narasimham

CRESCENT
PUBLISHING CORPORATION

[*The responsibility for the facts stated, conclusions reached and plagiarism, if any, in this book is entirely that of the Author. And the Publisher bears no responsibility for them, whatsoever.*]

Planning and Control of Sports Training

First Published : 2009

ISBN 978-81-8342-119-5

Published by :

CRESCENT PUBLISHING CORPORATION
4831/24, Prahlad Street,
Ansari Road, Darya Ganj,
New Delhi - 110002
Ph. : 23272541, 23257835
Fax : 91- 011- 23257835
e-mail : campusbooks@hotmail.com

Printed at :
Roshan Offset Printers
Delhi

Preface

Sports in the Indian culture has undergone dramatic changes. During colonial days, few people engaged in highly organised sports. As the nation became industrialised, sports played a more important part in the Indian society. The growth of sports in educational institutions has also undergone change. If this change on a grand scale is to be achieved without violent revolution there is one instrument only, that can be used: education and training. The national system of education is the only instrument that can reach all the youth.

The National Policy on Education identified two key areas namely Integration of sports in the learning process and evaluation of performance and involvement of youth in national and social development through educational institutions. Reconstruction in the area of sports became a necessity. The government of India is taking initiatives in the organization and expansion of sports in general and developing the youth physically, mentally and socially useful citizens in particular.

This book *Planning and Control of Sports Training* will go a long way in helping physical education teachers and coaches to tackle specific problems of in planning a training programme. The language used is simple and is within the comprehension level of teachers and students pursuing career in physical and sports.

T.K. Narasimham

Contents

	Preface	*v*
1.	Developing a Sports Training Programme	1
2.	Training Technologies	29
3.	Planning for Strength Training	52
4.	Planning of Speed and Agility Training'	102
5.	Designing an Effective Speed Training Programme	127
6.	Planning and Control of Athletic Training	145
7.	Nutrition Planning	187
8.	Training Plan for Swimmers	233
9.	Planning for Success	250
10.	Performance Evaluation	257
	Bibliography	295
	Index	297

1

Developing a Sports Training Programme

The process of creating a training programme to help develop an individual's level of fitness comprises of 6 stages:

— Stage 1 - gather details about the individual
— Stage 2 - identify the fitness components to develop
— Stage 3 - identify appropriate tests to monitor fitness status
— Stage 4 - conduct a gap analysis
— Stage 5 - compile the program
— Stage 6 - monitor progress and adjust program

Stage 1

The first stage is to gather details about the individual:

— Age
— Reasons for wanting to get fit
— Current or recent injuries
— Health problems
— The sports they play and how often

— Their dislikes and likes with regards training
— What sports facilities they have access to - gym, sports centre etc.

Prior to starting any training, it is recommended you have a medical examination to ensure it is safe for you to do so.

Stage 2

The second stage is to determine that components of fitness they need to improve. This could depend upon what the individual wants to get fit for. This could be to improve general fitness, get fit enough to play in the Saturday hockey league, run a local 5 km fun run or compete in next year's London Marathon.

Exercise scientists have identified nine elements that comprise the definition of fitness. The following lists each of the nine elements and an example of how they are used:

— *Strength* - the extent to which muscles can exert force by contracting against resistance (holding or restraining an object or person)
— *Power* - the ability to exert maximum muscular contraction instantly in an explosive burst of movements (Jumping or sprint starting)
— *Agility* - the ability to perform a series of explosive power movements in rapid succession in opposing directions (ZigZag running or cutting movements)
— *Balance* - the ability to control the body's position, either stationary (e.g. a handstand) or while moving (e.g. a gymnastics stunt)
— *Flexibility* - the ability to achieve an extended range of motion without being impeded by excess tissue, i.e. fat or muscle (Executing a leg split)

— *Local Muscle Endurance* - a single muscle's ability to perform sustained work (Rowing or cycling)

— *Cardiovascular Endurance* - the heart's ability to deliver blood to working muscles and their ability to use it

— *Strength Endurance* - a muscle's ability to perform a maximum contracture time after time.

— *Coordination* - the ability to integrate the above listed components so that effective movements are achieved.

Of all the nine elements of fitness cardiac respiratory qualities are the most important to develop as they enhance all the other components of the conditioning equation. You will need to consider which of these elements are applicable to the individuals training program based on what it is they want to get fit for.

Stage 3

The next stage is to identify appropriate tests that can be used to initially determine the individual's level of fitness and then to monitor progress during the training. The Evaluation Test page identifies suitable tests for each of the fitness elements. Identified test should be conducted and the results recorded.

Stage 4

We now know the individual's background, objectives and current level of fitness. We now need to conduct a gap analysis of the current fitness levels and target fitness levels. The results of this process will assist in the design of the training program so that each component of fitness is improved to the desired level. The following table is an example of a gap analysis:

Test	Fitness Component	Current	Target
Multistage Fitness Test	Aerobic	Level 12 Shuttle 2	Level 12 Shuttle 5
30 metre acceleration Test	Speed	4.3 seconds	3.9 seconds
Illinois agility run Test	Agility	20 seconds	<16 seconds
Standing Long Jump Test	Leg power	2.4 metres	2.8 metres
Over head medicine ball throw	Arm power	16.1 metres	16 metres

Gap analysis - Aerobic fitness and arm power are good and just need to be maintained - sprint, agility and leg power tests are below target - leg power needs to be improved.

Stage 5

The next stage is to prepare a training program using the results of the gap analysis and FITT principles.

— *F-frequency* - how often should the individual exercise?

— *I-intensity* - how hard should the individual exercise?

— *T-time* - how long should each session last?

— *T-training activity* - what exercise or training activity will help achieve the individual's fitness goals?

For frequency, intensity and time you should start at an easy level and increase gradually e.g. 10% increments. Aerobic training should last for 20 to 40 minutes. Strength work should last 15 to 30 minutes and comprise of 3 sessions a week with 48 hours recovery between sessions.

Plan the program in four week cycles where the workload in the first three weeks increase each week (easy, medium, hard) and the fourth week comprises of active recovery and tests to monitor training progress.

The aim of the four week cycles is to:

— Build you up to a level of fitness (3 weeks)
— Test, recovery and adjustment of the training program (1 week)
— Build you up to higher level of fitness (3 weeks)
— Test, recovery and adjustment of the training program (1 week)
— Build you up to an even higher level of fitness (3 weeks)
— and so on

The tests used to assess the individual's initial level of fitness should be planned into week 4 of the program in order to monitor progress and effectiveness of the program. The test results can be used to adjust the program accordingly.

The program needs to last 12 to 16 weeks in order to see any real benefits and the planning should be conducted with the individual so that they feel they own the program. This will ensure the program is enjoyable and convenient to do.

Stage 6

The program has now been agreed and the individual can undertake the program. Every 4 weeks meet and discuss with the individual:

— how the training has gone
— the test results
— progress towards target fitness levels
— adjustments to the training program

The following are example training programs:

— Develop general fitness for team sports

— Develop general strength using dumbbells
— Training to run a marathon

Make a plan and stick to it

Getting fit is a journey, and to successfully complete a journey you often need a map. By planning how to get from A to B, we can prepare for change and give ourselves a route to follow which will allow us to progress along our chosen path without having to worry about losing our way or getting distracted. Remember the old adage - "prior preparation prevents poor performance!" To help keep on the straight and narrow, consider the following points:

— Plan your workout times - treat them as appointments and stick to them.
— Have a back up plan in case you are unable to exercise at the time you wanted to - if you cant go to the gym, what can you do instead? If it is raining, where else can you workout? Cover your bases! Have alternatives ready to cover as many eventualities as you can envisage.
— Plan your weekly food intake and shop accordingly. One of the truths of diet and nutrition is that if you have junk food in your cupboard, you will eat it. As a result, make sure that you have plenty of healthy food in your cupboards and that includes snacks.
— Make sure you carry adequate food and water with you so you do not have to rely on grabbing a snack at work - prepare much of your days food the night before
— Tell other people about your plans so they do not accidentally interfere with your efforts to adopt a new healthy lifestyle.

Recruit a network of supporters

Why suffer alone? Ask friends, neighbors, family and friends to assist you in your goals. Seek out like minded people to act as training partners, get support from those closest to you, join one of the many web based groups that can offer both support and information to help you on your way. The main point is that you do not have to "go it alone". For some people this might mean hiring a personal trainer, or joining a group exercise class or it could just mean you work out with a neighbor. Whatever support method you choose, your efforts will be easier with someone else in your corner.

Keep accurate training and diet logs

Write it down! Nothing motivates like success..but to judge success we need to see where we started. By keeping track of workout performance, dietary trends and physical measurements we can see when we improve. Sometimes we fail to see our improvements because they are, on a day to day basis, so small but overtime, these small improvements will add up to noticeable changes in body composition, bodyweight, fitness levels etc. Often, someone who has not seen you for a while will comment on your dramatic weight loss or improved muscle tone - they have not seen you in a while so the changes seem great whereas to you, seeing yourself in the mirror on a daily basis may not have spotted much in the way of changes at all.

Even with the very best planning, goal setting and support network sometimes things just go wrong - life gets in the way. The key when this happens is to not let it phase you for too long and to pick up where you left off as soon as possible. These disruptions in routine are not failures, nor are they enough to undo all of your previous good works but unless you jump back on the wagon as soon as possible, they can be the start of the slippery slope back to our previous physical state and a lot of hard work wasted. Learn from whatever caused this disruption to your planned routine and take measures to try to minimize the chances of a similar disruptions happening again. Its kind of cheesy but some say that to fail is the First Action in Learning and so long as we take something positive away from a failure, then it was not a wasted opportunity.

Choose things you like

By using the above 6 points, we can make exercise adherence much more likely, but if we choose activities we do not enjoy or foods we do not like, it becomes increasingly doubtful we will succeed in reaching our fitness or diet goals. There are many options for us to choose from and it is vital we chose things we are going to enjoy as much as possible. Why make things harder than they need to be? The old saying "it does not have to be hell to be healthy" is a good one to adopt as a diet and exercise mantra. So..do not like running? Try cycling. Not so keen on the gym? Join an exercise class. Do not like fruit? Make fresh fruit smoothies or juices. There are many ways to skin the proverbial cat, so spread you net wide and select activities and foods that slot as seamlessly into your lifestyle as possible.

Planning your athlete's training is essential

Planning of an athlete's training program is essential if both short and long term objectives are to be achieved at the right time in the season.

Training plan

The purpose of a Training Plan is to identify the work to be carried out to achieve agreed objectives. Training Plans should be drawn up to identify long term (4 years) objectives as well as short term plans for the forth coming season. For the rest of this topic I will concentrate on the development of the short term annual Training Plan. In its simplest form the plan could comprise of a single, A4 sheet identifying the overall plan for the year, and more detailed weekly plans identifying the specific activities the athlete is to carry out.

Training year

The start of the training year will depend upon the athletes circumstances and objectives, but this would generally be around October for track and field athletics.

Information gathering

The first stage of preparing a Training Plan is to gather background information about your athlete and the objectives for the forth coming season. The sort of information to collect is as follows :

— Personal details

— Name, address, date of birth, telephone numbers, transport arrangements

— Objectives

— Performance (time, height, distance)

— Technical (development of event technique)

— Indoor and/or outdoor season

— Experience

— Personal best (PB's)

— Competition experience (club, county, national, country)

— Equipment

  — Does the athlete have his own equipment (e.g. starting blocks, javelin etc.)?

- — Harness and tyre
- — Elastic harness
- — Weight jackets
- — Video Camera
- — Distance, time, % effort matrix chart

— Finance

- — Where can grants be obtained from?

— Competition

- — Date of main competition
- — National and Area Championships
- — School, University competitions
- — Required qualification times for competitions

— Fixture lists - Club, County etc.

— Open Meetings

— Competitors

- — Who are the competition and what are their PB's?

— Recent competition results

— Competition behaviour

— Athlete's other Commitments

- — School, college, work, part time jobs
- — Family and partner
- — Hobbies and other sports

— Time available for training

— Planned holidays

— Medical

- — Previous injuries or illness
- — Current problems (diabetes, asthma etc.)

  - Access to medical support
  - Physiotherapy support
  - On any medication - is it a banned substance ?
  - Using asthma inhaler - application to use Beta 2 agent inhalers
- Training facilities
  - Tracks and other running facilities (bad weather)
  - Gymnasiums and weight training
  - Swimming pools, saunas and massage
- Coaching Workshops
- Last season
  - What can be learnt from last season - good and bad aspects
- Key questions for the athlete
  - How serious are you about your athletics ?
  - What do expect from your coach ?

Periodisation

It is the method of organising the training year into phases where each phase has its specific aims for the development of the athlete.

The phases of a training year

The training year is divided into 6 phases as follows:

- Phase 1 - 16 weeks - Oct, Nov, Dec, Jan
- Phase 2 - 8 weeks - Feb, Mar
- Phase 3 - 8 weeks - Apr, May
- Phase 4 - 8 weeks - Jun, Jul
- Phase 5 - 8 weeks - Jul, Aug
- Phase 6 - 4 weeks - Sep

What if there is an indoor and an outdoor season ?

For the athlete with competitive objectives for both the indoor and outdoor season then the phase allocation for the indoor season could be as follows :

— Phase 1 - 6 weeks - Oct, Nov

— Phase 2 - 8 weeks - Nov, Dec, Jan

— Phase 3 - 6 weeks - Jan, Feb

and the outdoor season as follows :

— Phase 1 - 4 weeks - Feb, Mar

— Phase 2 - 6 weeks - Mar, Apr

— Phase 3 - 5 weeks - Apr, May

— Phase 4 - 7 weeks - Jun, Jul

— Phase 5 - 6 weeks - Jul, Aug

— Phase 6 - 4 weeks - Sep

This assumes that the climax of the indoor season is in February and the outdoor season in August. Depending on your athlete's objectives and abilities, then the year start and duration of each phase may have to be adjusted to achieve appropriate development.

Objectives of each phase

The objectives of each phase are as follows :

— Phase 1 - General development of strength, mobility, endurance and basic technique

— Phase 2 - Development of specific fitness and advanced technical skills

— Phase 3 - Competition experience - achievement of indoor objectives

— Phase 4 - Adjustment of technical model, preparation for the main competition

— Phase 5 - Competition experience and achievement of outdoor objectives

— Phase 6 - Active recovery - planning preparation for next season

Activities of each phase

The athlete's physical needs that .require development are:

— Basic body Conditioning

— General and Specific Strength

— General and Specific Technique

— General and Specific Mobility

— General and Specific Endurance

— Speed

Each of these needs should be seen as a building block, where specific blocks need to be in place before you progress to the next. Failure to do this may result in injury. How you allocate the blocks to each phase depends upon the athlete's weaknesses and strengths and is for you as the coach to decide with the athlete.

One approach is to progress the building blocks as follows:

— basic body conditioning

— general strength, endurance, mobility and technique

— specific strength, endurance, mobility and technique

— speed

When progressing from one block to the next, remember to fade one out as the other comes in and not to switch from one block to the next overnight. Some blocks once started may continue to the end of the season but at a less intense level e.g. mobility.

Preparing a plan

The steps in producing a Training Plan are as follows:

- Gathering information
- Produce an overall plan template and identify the months/weeks of the year
- Identify on the plan at the appropriate period
  - the main competition
  - area, national, school etc. championships
  - qualification competitions
  - club fixture meetings
  - the 6 phases based on the main competition in phase 5
- Identify on the plan
  - the blocks (e.g. strength, endurance) to be developed in each phase
  - the period of development for each block
  - the intensity of training week by week
  - number of training sessions per week
  - evaluation points to monitor progress
- Identify appropriate training units for each block as appropriate to the phase of development.
- Group the training units for each block into training schedules taking into consideration the number of training sessions the athlete can complete per week, the required training intensity and the phase of development.

What are a training unit and a training session ?

A training unit is a single activity (e.g. 6x60m at 90% effort with 2 min recovery) with a set objective (e.g. develop specific endurance). A training session is made up of one or more training units e.g. warm up unit,

Technique drills unit, Speed Endurance unit and a cool down unit.

What is a training schedule?

A training schedule (microcycle) comprises of a number of training units that can span from 7 to 30 days.

What are a microcycle, mesocycle and marcrocycle

A microcycle, also known as a training schedule, is a group of training units. The mesocycle, also known as a macrocycle, is a number of repeats of a microcycle.

Goal setting is a simple, yet often misused motivational technique which can provide some structure for your training and competition programme. Goals give a focus, and there are two well known acronyms to guide goal setting.

SMART or SMARTER

— S - goals must be Specific
— M - training targets should be Measurable
— A - goals should be Adjustable
— R - goals must be Realistic
— T - training targets should be Time based
— E - goals should be challenging and Exciting
— R - goals should be Recorded

SCCAMP

— S - goals must be Specific
— C - within the Control of the athlete
— C - goals are Challenging
— A - goals must be Attainable

— M - training targets should be Measurable

— P - goals are Personal

FITT Principles

The basic principles of fitness training are summed up in the acronym FITT.

— F - Frequency - how often

— I - Intensity - how hard

— T - Time - how long

— T - Type - the type of training (strength, endurance etc.)

Knowing at what age an athlete is likely to achieve peak performance is a big help in planning a training programme

An 800 metre and 1500 metre male runner is most likely to run his fastest at around the age of 25. If you don't believe it, compare the ages of past and present world record holders for these distances. For females, the peak is delayed to the age of 27. Why women differ in this regard is a mystery. There are, of course, exceptions to the rule but these are rare. In addition, having achieved an all time best time at these ages, the athletes often continue for another decade with world class times. Seb Coe, for example, ran 1:41.73 for 800 metres at age 24 and 1:43.52 for 800 metres at age 33. Steve Cram ran a mile in 3:46:32 aged 25, and 3:53.8 when he was 30. The age at which a male runner is most likely to run a lifetime best for 3K and 5K is 27, for females, 29. For the 10k, it is 29 and 31, respectively.

What is the significance of these statistics?

First of all, they tell the 14-year-old keen club runner that he or she has a long way to go before they reach true potential. Parents of such athletes who want to see their offspring on the Olympic podium in their teens have little chance of seeing that dream fulfilled. These statistics point the way to changing the competitive distance to a longer one. Moving up a distance before the indicated age is not a good idea. All longer distance events are associated with what the athlete has achieved at a shorter one. For instance, the calculation for running a 5K is three times the 1500 metre time plus 2.5 minutes e.g., best 1500 metre time=4 min 5k=4 min x 3 + 2.5 min=14 min 30 sec At world class level add 2.25 minutes e.g. best 1500 metre time=3:40 min x 3 + 2.25 min=13 min 15 sec. The same applies to the 10k distance. This is usually calculated at twice the 5K time plus one minute e.g. best 5K=14 min 10k=14 min x 2 + 1 min=29 min. In order to run sub 27 minutes for the 10k an athlete would need to have a time of around 3:30 min for 1500 metres, which indicates a 13 min/5K, which makes a sub 27 min/10k a possibility. The age of peak performance in the marathon is between 30 and 37 years of age. This, too, is largely dependent on what the athlete has done at 10k. A rule-of-thumb indicator is five times the 10k time equals the potential marathon time e.g., best 10k time=30 min - marathon=2 hrs 30 min.

This is considered a little pessimistic by some and optimistic by others, however, by adding plus or minus five minutes to this original formula, we won't go far wrong.

	10k	Marathon
Emil Zatopek	28 min 54.00 sec	2 hr 23 min 32 sec
Liz McColgan	30 min 57:07 sec	2 hr 27 min 32 sec
Eamonn Martin	27 min 23:06 sec	2 hr 10 min 50 sec

Hanging in there

The other quality that age statistics give to an athlete is patience. I recall a 24 year old Royal Marine miler who was stuck at 4:08 min for the 1500 metres, which he had done four times. A new coach took him in hand and at the age of 25 he ran a 3:56 min/mile. He also broke the UK 1500 metre record (3:38.78) in 1972. This runner was on the point of giving up athletics at the age of 24! An apt saying to remember when progress seems to slow down at this crucial time is: "Keep on, keep on, until a little something inside you says 'KEEP ON!'"

Time for action

The age allowance also permits the athlete and coach to assess personal strengths and weaknesses and gives time for concrete action to be taken. Here is an example. Paula is a 22-year-old club runner with personal best times of 4 min 40 sec 1500 metre, 2 min 12 sec 800 metre, and 56 sec 400 metre.

What do these times tell us?

If we apply the 5-second rule for females, we get some fascinating results. This rule is when 5 seconds per 400 metres is added to the distances above. For instance, 2:12/800 metres is 66 seconds per lap, but if we add 5 seconds to her 400 metres time of 56 seconds it equals 61 seconds, and if multiplied by two it equals a potential of 2:02 for 800 metres (61 seconds per 400 metres). If we take this further, her 1500 metres time should be 66 seconds per 400 metres (4 min: 7.05 sec). Quite clearly, this athlete has not achieved her potential, but why? Her 400 metre time is good, but her 800 metre time is double the 5 second rule instead of being able to run two consecutive laps of 61 seconds (56 + 5), she can only run 56 seconds + 10 seconds (2:12). Further, she can only run 74.5 seconds per lap in the 1500 metres, where her potential is 66 seconds per 400 metres, some 8.5 seconds faster. As the event distance increases, she gets proportionately slower.

She obviously lacks endurance for the longer distances beyond 400 metres.

What must be done?

First of all, she will have to start training at these new speeds on a regular basis. She will have to inoculate herself with these speeds consistently, so that when experienced in races they will not come as an unwelcome shock. So, she could train at 1500 metre speed on Sunday, 800 metre pace on Tuesday and 400 metre speed on Thursday. On the days between these track sessions, she could bind together the speed sessions with the steady runs.

Reducing recovery times

At this point it is wise to remember the old Chinese maxim: "A 10,000 mile walk starts with the first step". The main task is to get used to the new speeds, which means adequate recovery times after repetitions. This recovery must be reduced gradually as the times are achieved. Here is a table of starting times with progressions:

— 1500 metre speed - 8 x 400 metre in 66 sec with 400 metre jog recovery (3 min). Reducing the 400-metre jog by 100 metre (45 sec) to 300 metres, then to 200 metres (90 sec)

— 800 metre speed - 8 x 200 metres in 30 sec with 200 metre jog recovery (90 sec). Reducing to 100-metre jog (45 sec) when achieved

— 400 metre speed - 1 x 350 metres full out, jog 800 metres (6 min), 1 x 300 metres full out, jog 800 metres, 1 x 250 metres full out, jog 800 metres, 1 x 200 metres full out. Reducing the jog recovery in stages by 100 metres until 400 metres (3 min)

As these distances are achieved, they can be increased to bear a relationship to the actual race distances. e.g. 1500 metres speed, 4 x 800 metres in 2:12 with 400 metres jog recovery (3 min). 800 metres speed, 4 x 400 metres in 61 sec, 400 metres jog recovery (3 min). In place of early preparation races, meaningful time trials over segments of the race distance can be done. Traditional favourites are 1200 metres for the 1500 metres, 600 metres for the 800 metres and 300 metres for the 400 metres.

The implication of this analogy is that a minimum of four races is required at any distance to bring about minimum results. This would be four of each at 400 metres, 800 metres and 1500 metres. Many will find that double this number may be needed. In the US there is a preference to racing under distance more than the specialist distance. Thus an 800 metre specialist would race, say, eight 400 metres races and only four at 800 metres. There is a psychological advantage in preceding a longer race with a shorter one e.g. 400 metres followed by 800 metres; 800 metres followed by 1500 metres; 1500 metres followed by a 3K or 5K. There would, of course, be a week or a fortnight's gap between such races.

What I said about lack of endurance in the example applies equally to lack of speed. There is often an air of hopelessness about not being fast at 400 metres. One thing is for sure, if regular sprint work is not done, it will not improve. There is also a right and a wrong way to sprint. Leg strength is a vital ingredient in a sprinter. One simple test is the number of hops needed to cover 25 metres; 10 hops on each leg are indicative of good leg strength for sprinting. If an athlete is way off this target, regular hopping exercises and/or judicious weight training under expert supervision can develop it. As leg strength improves so does the stride length, and provided the strike rate remains the same, the athlete will automatically go faster.

How to Squash in the Training

Then, as their standard improves, they find they need to get fit to play squash. Running around the court for 40 minutes or an hour will certainly give you a useful workout and improve your fitness if you do it regularly. However, there usually comes a time when to be competitive you need to do a bit of extra work, whether you aim to win the British Open, win your club league, or simply thrash your old sparring partner in your weekly duel.

Demands of the sport

Because of its constant whole-body activity, squash is a sport that demands a high level of aerobic fitness. In a typical game, you will be working at about 80% of your maximum heart rate as you pounce from corner to corner and back to the T for the next shot. Although the distance traveled in each movement is short and explosive, the continuous nature of the rallies with recovery periods in between means that the energy supply comes from aerobic metabolism. This does not mean that you have to run hundreds of miles in training, because there are other fitness demands in the game as well.

It is important to have speed in order to be able to pick up your opponent's craftiest backhand drop shot and get back in position after your reply. Anaerobic endurance is also an essential fitness requirement. During long, heart bursting rallies the ability to keep going at high intensity is critical, and this relies on solid local muscular endurance, particularly in the legs.

Muscular strength is important for both the lower and upper body. Strong legs will contribute to anaerobic fitness, while strong arms, chest and back will help with racket speed and power. Toning of the muscles in the back, abdominals and legs will also enhance good posture on court. It is also essential to have a full range of movements in the muscles you are using, since agility is vital in a game with so many rapid shifts of direction. This means that sound flexibility is crucial not only to a match performance but also in helping prevent injury.

Phases of training

The main playing season in the UK covers the winter months. Therefore, the summer is the ideal time to pack in some conditioning training. Development work on both strength and endurance is the way to make significant gains in fitness and provide a base to be maintained during the playing season.

Always remember that it is not sensible to be training hard just when you want to play at your best, so you may need to build your program towards the matches that really matter to you. This will mean more endurance work at the start of the program, followed by work on anaerobic endurance using more shorter speed work towards the key competition period. To be at your best when it really counts means you have to phase the fitness training. Bringing yourself to a planned peak is a great way to impress friends and shock opponents.

The training week

Because squash carries such a wide range of fitness requirements, the best prepared players will have a varied training program. The proportion of the different sessions will change throughout the year. To develop aerobic endurance it is best to do some steady state running. Cycling and swimming will help to condition the heart and lungs, but remember that you play squash on your feet! For base endurance, you can do a long slow run of up to an hour one day, then on another day try a 20-30 minute faster effort. If you do not do much running normally, be sure to build up gradually.

Court sprints are a useful way to boost anaerobic endurance. They involve running a series of lengths of the court at a fast pace and then resting briefly before repeating. This type of work does not have to be done on a court at all, many top players undertake a lot of short sprints on the track. You can vary the distances with each session, giving yourself sprints over 30 or 60 metres.

For specific speed work on court, ghosting is a useful routine whereby you run at random (get a partner to call) to different parts of the court. The key here is to keep the efforts short an the recovery sufficient to maintain good quality. Work in the gym, lifting weights or bodyweight, is an excellent way to develop strength and should be fitted into the schedule. In the meantime, do not forget stretching before and after all sessions, to prepare for and recover from exercise, although dedicated flexibility sessions are useful if time allows. All this, of course, needs to be adding to your playing time on court! Realistically, do not make this a flat out match every time. Structured practice sessions are essential, either on your own or with a partner. It is also useful to have a variety of matches in your schedule, easy ones to perfect your killing shot, medium and hard ones to practice playing under pressure.

Tapering for Success

Most endurance athletes accept that tapering before a competition is beneficial, but few understand why.

A trial was conducted back in the 1980's by a group of Canadian researchers at the McMaster University in Ontario. The trial was conducted for a one week period, with a group of experienced endurance athletes who all run approximately 50 miles a week in training. The athletes were split into 3 groups, with each group working a different training programme for the week. At the end of the week the performance improvement for each group was checked. The results were as follows:

Group	*Training programme*	*% reduction intraining load*	*% improvement*
1	No training	100%	0%
2	18 miles (easy running)	64%	6%
3	6 miles (500m sessions at max effort)	88%	22%

As it can be seen from the table, group 3 achieved the best improvement in their performance (22%). In addition group 3 enjoyed four advantages over the other groups

— More glycogen in the leg muscles
— Increased density of red blood cells
— Increased blood plasma
— Increased enzyme activity in their leg muscles

Similar tests have also concluded that as well as achieving the above advantages there is also an improvement in the neural system. The end result is that the athlete has an improved ability of a better rested nervous system to control and co-ordinate better rested muscles at faster running speeds. These are all very desirable in an athlete's preparation for a major competition.

Tapering in training

If tapering in this way can have this effect on your performance then perhaps you should consider including tapering weeks in your season's training programs. In this fourth week the training load is reduced by 70%, 2 or 3 tests at max effort are performed and light sessions are included between tests. The tests are used to monitor progress made in the proceeding three weeks of training and the results are considered in the planning of the next 4 week cycle.

How to Design and Plan Successful Training Phases

A training phase could be anything from a few weeks to many weeks long and is usually characterised as being part of an overall series of sequential or partially overlapping phases called a 'period' aimed at attaining a specific performance goal. Traditionally, coaches use names such as 'general conditioning', 'specific conditioning' or 'pre-competition' to describe phases. These suggest many possible activities but tend not to be very enlightening. Of more practical help to the coach and athlete may be to consider what the intermediate goals are for each phase, how to identify them and what to do to achieve them.

Planning

Predominantly, we are concerned with training one or more of the fitness components - speed, strength, endurance, flexibility and skill - all of these can be trained and all can be trained in various sub-categories e.g. maximal strength / core strength. The key to success is working on the basis that it is firstly important to identify what needs to be improved, by how much and why. Furthermore, consider how we will be able to measure the improvement and understand the timescales involved - e.g. it will typically take 6 to 8 weeks to train a consistent and measurable improvement and often longer to achieve the desired goal. We also need to consider how this change may impact on other factors e.g. strength gains may cause a specific reduction in flexibility unless worked on in parallel. The following is an example of an intermediate goal improve flexibility in lower back / hamstrings over a 12 week period by more than 12cm, measured with the 'sit and reach test', to reduce occurrence of chronic tightness in these areas. Initial test result: 28cm; goal: 40cm; ultimate goal: 48cm. Examples of (stretching) activities (seek expert guidance if not certain).

— Seated hamstring stretch - knee partially flexed

— Standing hamstring stretch - feet wide apart; bending forward at waste aiming to achieve back parallel to ground with arms in alignment with back.

— Lateral stretch (sideways) from waist with feet wide apart and sliding hand down leg while bringing opposite arm over top of head.

How much and how long:

— 20 to 30 second static hold in stretched position

— 3 to 5 sets of 8 to 10 stretches each performed 3 to 5 times per week for a minimum of 6 weeks.

To achieve optimum results the programme should be progressive in terms of the number of stretches performed in a given session and the number of session per week.

Warm up thoroughly before performing any stretches. You should not be fatigued when stretching. Treat this as a training session in itself and perform it in a warm, comfortable environment. Gently cool down afterwards. Do not overstretch; pain should not be experienced during stretching.

Measure progress using the sit and reach test every two weeks. Reassess goal after 6 weeks and relative success of measures employed. Record all sessions! Devise a maintenance program once goal is achieved. Setting intermediate goals for athletes can be highly motivating in terms of achieving meaningful results without exposing them, for example, to the rigours of competition.

Without a Plan, you will be Mediocre at Best

The most common problem facing Trainers & Coaches today with respect to developing young athletes over time is the ability to plan long-term. The personal training and coaching professions are most typically based on a session-to-session consideration - clients pay per session most often and Trainers create training programs one session at a time. The same is true for coaching sport - most Coaches script out one practice plan at a time, rather than create a relative flow for an entire month or even season.

Limited plan... Limited gain

The problem with this industry standard as it relates to youths and adolescents is that this type of short sightedness serves to limit the potential gains made by a young athlete. It is not unlike running a business or corporation - when business owners take the time to organize their objectives and action steps for a given month or year, they almost always are successful at implementing the plan. Far too many Trainers and Coaches feel as though their actions during a training session or practice is what will lead to positive change, when in fact it is the planning that occurs before these actions that accounts for the true gains.

Become an Objective Monster

No one can learn how to create 6 or 12 month plans in a day. It takes time and diligent effort to acquire this skill, but your ability to get better over time will have a direct and positive impact on both your young athletes' success rate as well as your businesses/teams ability to attract new clients. Set an objective for yourself to create a system or plan that allows you to develop long-term and wide-focused agendas for your young athletes. Take several days or weeks if need be to create a system that is streamlined and easy to implement - although your are looking for a comprehensive system, the more basic you make it, the more easy it will be to adhere to.

Create Critical Path

Once you have organized your thoughts on where you would like to be in 4 weeks, you have to consider how you are going to get there. On the same or a different piece of paper, right out how many training sessions or practices you have with this athlete or team between now and 4 weeks from now. Date each training session or practice on your piece of paper. Now, using your skills as a Trainer or Coach, literally, just fill in the blanks. Compare where you want to be in 4 weeks with the number of training sessions or practices you have between now and then. In order to accomplish your 4 week goal, what action steps along a critical path must be taken? This is the essence of how to develop a long-term approach to working with young athletes. You will simply just write out your next several training sessions or practices in order to meet the objectives you have set for 4 weeks from now.

2

Training Technologies

In a modern sport, performance improvement depends upon proper levels of physical, technical, psychological and tactical preparedness of the athlete. Different means and methods exist to achieve this high level of preparedness.

It is widely accepted that adaptation is one of the main forms of the existence of living things. In essence this term refers to human being's general biological ability to adapt to various external and internal stresses. The human being, interacting with nature, changes his own nature. We monitor this phenomenon in a sporting practice every day. Affecting the organism's systems by a certain combination of training loads, we cause corresponding changes in a specific direction. Each adaptation process may lead to several purposeful changes both in the organism's whole system and separate muscle groups. Through the adaptation processes the athlete's body systems are balanced in external and internal environment. The organism exists while it can adapt to the surrounding environment. As soon as this balance is broken the organism does not exist anymore.

The state of balance is achieved through adaptation, which goes on throughout the whole life. Thus, adaptation is necessary because humans cannot live without this process. In a sporting practice, adaptation processes occur as follows: in a given time period the coach suggests to athlete one or other combinations of training loads, to which an athlete adapts to after some time. In other words, the athlete changes his corresponding body systems, enhancing his functional abilities.

Practically, sporting performances rise until the athlete's body is adapting to a certain combination of training effects. Adaptation to certain training combinations ends when an athlete obtains so-called athletic shape. This means that the body has adapted to given training loads. For further improvement of results it is necessary to reorganise the organism again. For that purpose, new and more efficient training means and methods have to be used in the training process.

Each stage of sporting perfection suits its own stage of adaptation. One combination of training loads is good for one level of sporting performance, but is inefficient for different performance levels. The degree of training affecting athlete's body systems has to increase with a higher level of athlete's performance.

Athletic Shape and its Criteria

Athletic shape is a state of optimal (best) readiness for sporting performance which is acquired under definite conditions in each big training cycle. The athletic shape as a whole represents harmonious unity of all components of the athlete's optimal readiness: physical, psychological, technical, and tactical. We can say that an athlete is in a state of athletic shape only when all these components are present. No matter how high an athlete's physical preparedness is and how perfect his technical and tactical skills are, he would not be able to demonstrate high performance in important competitions if the athlete does not have an adequate psychological preparedness. Therefore, athletic shape is characterised not only by the presence of various characteristics, but the harmonious ratio of the four parameters.

It is important to appreciate that the term optimal readiness is relative, in a sense it is part of a process of sporting perfection: it is correct for each given cycle of athletic shape development only. As the athlete improves results, this optimum changes - athletic shape becomes different in qualitative and quantitative aspects.

Real competition results are the main integral parameters of athletic shape. Only in sporting results we can see all aspects of the athlete's readiness for high performance. However, results are a significant parameter of athletic shape only when they are demonstrated with a definite frequency in comparable conditions and are evaluated objectively. Selection of qualitative criteria of athletic shape has an important theoretical and practical meaning. In this regard, studies have shown that there are two groups of such criteria: progress criteria and stability criteria.

Progress criteria characterise athletic shape by the degree of increment and absolute level of the athlete's performance in a given big cycle of training. Parameters here, in particular, might be:

1. Differences between the personal best achieved in a previous big cycle of training and the examined performance in a current cycle. The more the latter is better than the previous cycle's result, the greater the possibility that the athlete is in a state of athletic shape and vice versa. However, the athlete's training record and his personal best results have to be considered. Athletes with a long training record and an outstanding personal best result often have no

increment in their performance level in a given big cycle of training. Repetition of the athlete's personal best result, or a result close to personal best can be a conditional criterion of athletic shape.

2. The difference between the considered result of a control competition and results of first competitions in a given big training cycle: the more the athlete exceeds his results shown in first competitions, the greater the possibility that the athlete is near a state of his athletic shape.

Following parameters can be considered as stability criteria:

1. The number of results demonstrated by an athlete within a so-called rated zone of athletic shape. The lower limit of this zone must not greatly deviate from the personal best result for the high class athlete. For example, in cyclic sporting events (excluding long distances) the lower limit of a zone of athletic shape is a result, which is about 98 to 98.5% of a personal best result; in acyclic sporting events, the zone is not less than 95 to 97% of a personal best result. In other words, if an athlete shows results below this level, it speaks that an athlete is not in a state of athletic shape (he/she is out of shape). However, if the athlete's competition results are higher than a given level, that means he is in a state of athletic shape. Recent evidence suggests that high performance athletes manage to demonstrate up to 1/3 of all results within a given zone in the annual training cycle
2. The average time interval between results in a rated zone of athletic shape. The more the athlete can demonstrate such results in a given big training cycle and the shorter the time interval between them, the stability of athletic shape is much higher

3. The total duration of competitive period, during which sporting results with systematic participation in competitions do not drop below the level of the athletic shape zone.

These criteria are significant only if the athlete participates in competitions quite often. There are not informative if, for example, the athlete competes once a month; but they provide significant information if there are weekly competitions, which is typical for the competitive period of high performance athletes.

Since criteria of progress and the stability of athletic shape are characterised by different relations, the relationships between them are not uniform. The total number of competitions in a one big training cycle is usually correlated positively with the increment and absolute level of performance. However, the number of important competitions often has a negative correlation with these parameters. It is important to remember that the state of athletic shape can be determined only when all combination of criteria are used to evaluate separate characteristics of athlete's preparedness along with specialised methods of functional control (medical, biological, psychological).

Phases of Athletic Shape Development Recent evidence suggests that the process of athletic shape development has some different phases called acquisition, retention (or relative stabilisation) and temporary loss of athletic shape (Figure 1).

The first phase is the phase of the formation and improvement of conditions that are the basis of the state of athletic shape, and the first phase concludes with an integral system of specific components. At this stage the general level of athlete's body's functional abilities are increased together with a multilateral development of his/her physical and mental qualities, and the formation and perfection of necessary motor skills. It seems reasonable to assume that performance levels due to athletic shape depend firstly on the quality of its foundation.

The second phase is characterised by relative stabilisation of athletic shape as a system of components providing (ensuring) optimal readiness for sporting performances. Total restructuring of these components in a given phase is not possible, because this will lead to loss of athletic shape. However, with a process of athletic shape stabilisation there is a further perfection of all those factors, which are important for high sporting performances. That is why results grow in limits, which the regularities of the given athletic shape allow.

The variations of results at this stage of athletic shape are common (Figures 1, 2 and 3), that is because, on the one hand, the operative athlete's readiness is expediently regulated at the stages of his preparation and participation at different levels, and, on the other hand, the body's functional conditions periodically fluctuate at this particular stage. Such variations of results are not a sign of athletic shape loss (if, of course, their deterioration does not become a stable tendency).

The third phase is distinguished by changes of direction in adaptational processes, in the body's functional regime (rehabilitation, recuperation). Relationships and links, which acquired athletic shape and were stabilising earlier, are now weakened or destroyed partially. However, it does not mean that fundamental functions of the athlete's organism are violated. When athlete's general life regime and training regime are organised rationally (properly), the temporary loss of athletic shape does not affect the athlete's normal life activity.

Some athletes and coaches might ask: why can't an athlete be in a state of athletic shape permanently? In this regard, studies have shown that, firstly, athletic shape acquired at one or other stage of an athlete's sporting career is a state optimal for this given stage. For the next higher stage, this state is no more optimal. The athlete's desire to keep permanently a once acquired athletic shape would be similar to a desire to mark time. To advance, the athlete has to get rid of his old athletic shape and create conditions for the acquisition of a new athletic shape. This needs many more changes and improvements in all components of the athlete's preparedness.

Secondly, because of the prolonged effect of training and competitive loads, necessary for acquiring and stabilisation of athletic shape, the body's protective reaction is developed sooner or later to prevent overstraining of adaptation mechanisms. If a coach forgets about these factors, the same loads which led to athletic shape, would become stressors producing overtraining.

Thirdly, maintaining a complex dynamic balance between different biological functions and the processes guaranteeing athletic shape is already a hard task, especially the for athlete's central nervous system (CNS). This task becomes even more difficult, because it has to be resolved in a process of continual change of the organism's internal and external environment in the stressful conditions of sporting activity.

Thus, maintaining athletic shape is fraught with difficulties of both external and internal character. They might become excessive and lead to unpredictable consequences if an athlete tries to retain athletic shape for too long. However, it is not necessary. On the contrary, conservation of once acquired athletic shape would hinder the acquisition of a new athletic shape, i.e. it would be an obstacle to new performances.

Athletic Shape Maintenance

Many researchers studied the problem of the maintenance of athletic shape starting from the early 1930s. Different authors have various recommendations. Some authors advocate that it is necessary to increase the duration of the preparatory period between 2 to 6-7 months, because stability of adaptational changes depends upon both usage of a concrete combination of training loads and the length of their effects.

Former Soviet specialists designed so-called 'Principle of Pendulum' (PP). The Principle of Pendulum suggests the systematic alteration of two types of training microcycles - model-competitive and contrasting. The main aim of model-competitive microcycles is direct preparation for a main competition; and the aim of contrasting microcycles is compensation and super-compensation after competition. More specific exercises are used in the first type of microcycle; and less specialised and less intensive exercises in latter type of microcycles. In addition to model-competitive and contrasting microcycles there are so-called intermediate - developmental and maintenance microcycles. Thus, alteration of training means helps to maintain the athlete's athletic shape. In this regard, five different models of training have been studied at the retention phase of athletic shape.

— Maintenance of the same volume and intensity of training loads using the same training means
— Maintenance of volume with growth of intensity
— Lowering the volume (up to 50%) with growth of intensity
— Growth of volume (up to 50%) and intensity of training
— Change of training means (50%) and methods. Training intensity in models 2, 3 and 4 rose by 50%

Changes made to the training combination applied before the second acquisition of athletic shape helps to maintain the present level of athletic shape between 1 to 3 months; then the athlete loses the state of athletic shape. The duration of athletic shape retention in most cases do not exceed 2 months. Only in a few cases this period is either slightly shorter (1 month) or slightly longer (3 months). With the end of this period, the athlete has to change his training means, if there is an aim of further maintenance of athletic shape. Optimal duration of athletic shape retention for all athletes is 4 weeks. In one study, done by Bondarchuk, one of the experimental groups has been changing the combination of training means every 3 to 4 weeks. In this experiment, athletes could be in a state of athletic shape for as long as 5 months.

Athletes' individual characteristics in a process of athletic shape retention differ not only by duration of period of retention, but by direction of the fluctuations of sporting performance. Thus, in the first two weeks, one group of athletes improved their results after changes in a combination of training loads. In the next two weeks the tempo of improvement slightly decreased compared to the first two weeks. In a second group of athletes the opposite trend of the results were observed: in the first two weeks results were slightly lower; and in the following weeks improvement by several percent were observed. It seems reasonable to assume that there might be some other reactions of the athlete's body systems to changes in combinations of training loads (i.e., certain dynamics of sporting results).

Athletic shape maintenance becomes possible because of adaptational changes in the corresponding system of the body. It seems likely that the body, after a given time interval, receives new stimuli for further functioning in accordance with new external conditions. Active rest becomes very important for the recovery processes. Thus, active rest assists in athletic shape maintenance.

Temporary Loss of Athletic Shape

There are three phases of athletic shape development: acquisition, retention and temporary loss. The loss of athletic shape can be either of long term or of short term duration. The long term loss of athletic shape is observed in two cases:

— When an athlete is in a state of athletic shape and continues using the same combination of training means

— When an athlete excludes one or the other exercise from a training process for a certain time (from one to several months) during periods of either acquisition or retention of athletic shape

The loss of athletic shape in most cases is experienced by athletes after the transition period. At this time, results usually decrease by 5 to 10% (sometimes even more) compared to previous annual cycle results.

The short term loss of athletic shape can be observed in the second period of athletic shape development. The duration of the loss varies from 2 to 8 weeks. The short term reduction of performance levels during periods of athletic shape development after active or passive rest cannot be considered as a loss of athletic shape. This phenomenon is a part of the process of athletic shape development (adaptation processes to training loads is a basis of athletic shape development).

Duration of Periods of Athletic Shape Development

The time needed for certain athletes to obtain a state of athletic shape varies from one individual to another. From one perspective, it depends upon the functionality of individual characteristics of the athlete's body systems;

and, from the other side, it depends on incoming training effects and other factors. It should be pointed out that the duration of acquisition of athletic shape depends on an athlete's age. Thus, at the age of 20 to 30 years this period is normally 2 to 8 months. When an athlete becomes older period of athletic shape acquisition extends. The longer duration of acquisition of athletic shape happens because mechanisms of body systems' functioning change. This concerns not only CNS, but other systems as well (i.e., yielding of conditioned reflexes, chemical structure of the brain, etc.).

The duration of athletic shape development is increased with frequent alteration of training means, if a period of athletic shape acquisition starts after either active or passive rest. In some cases, periods of athletic shape acquisition might be longer when athletes use high volume training loads. These periods increase too when there are interruptions between training lessons, and micro and mesocycles of training (i.e., athlete's bad health condition). The time duration of preliminary general training (without usage of competitive exercise) does not affect (influence) the duration of athletic shape acquisition. The same is correct in the case of simple and complex coordination exercises.

Phases of Athletic Shape Development

The basic natural requirement for the periodisation of training process is the phase character or athletic shape development. Acquiring, stabilisation and temporary loss of athletic shape is a result of strictly defined training effects. The character of these effects regularly changes depending on phase of athletic shape development. There are three periods, which alternate in training:

— *Preparatory period.* During this period the foundation of athletic shape is formed

— *Competitive period.* During competitive period athletic shape has to be stabilised, retained and realised in sporting performances
— *Transition period,* which helps an athlete to regenerate the body's adaptation abilities and guarantee continuity between the two stages of athlete's training process.

It seems reasonable to assume that these periods are actually consecutive stages of controlling and managing the development of athletic shape. Objective possibilities allow manipulating the phases of its development, appropriately shortening or lengthening them. Naturally, any coach or athlete cannot limitlessly lengthen or shorten these phases, because, in general, their durations are determined by internal regularities of organism's development and depend on a number of specific conditions. The preparatory period, for example, cannot be shorter than it is necessary in given conditions for athletic shape acquirement. The competitive period must not be longer than what is allowed by the possibility of maintaining athletic shape. The length of transition period depends, first of all, upon total volume of preceding loads and a time necessary for the body's full rehabilitation.

The total duration of a big training cycle is often near to one year period. It is widely accepted that this time in many cases is quite enough for the development of athletic shape. However, in a number of sports (mainly in power or speed-strength dominated sports) the athletic shape can be renewed in the annual as well as in the semiannual cycles. Cycles, longer than annual, might be, in some cases, expedient, but needs more investigation.

Long term plan for young athletes

Coaches need to be aware that appropriate programming is necessary for improving performance but it is also essential for reducing the risk of injury to young athletes. Over training or incorrect training programming can be a contributing factor to many injuries in young athletes. When developing a season or annual training plan for young athletes, there is a very basic process that can be followed to ensure that consideration is taken to minimise many of the factors which could bring about injuries.

Developing an annual/seasonal training plan for school age athletes

— *Step 1:* Identify the major events that the athletes must peak for. Include any important dates in the plan including training camps, school holidays and exams.

— *Step 2:* Work chronologically backwards from this date outlining the weeks and months to the current date.

— *Step 3:* Divide the plan into three major training phases of a training plan (preparation, pre-competition, and competition)

— *Step 4:* Break each phase into the desired macro cycles and micro cycles incorporating appropriate loading and unloading (recovery) periods. A general recommendation for young school age athletes is to have a three-week macro cycle where you have two weeks of loading followed by one week unloading or recovery.

— *Step 5:* Determine target training load percentages for each phase.

— *Step 6:* Incorporate a method of monitoring the progress of the athletes into the plan, e.g. time trials, fitness tests, game rehearsals etc.

Designing a weekly plan for school age athletes

This process is recommended more for senior athletes, as junior athletes should be emphasising technical development.

— *Step 1:* Identify which phase the particular week occurs in and observe the target training load percentages for that phase

— *Step 2:* Observe the number of minutes, distance or performance target for that week

— *Step 3:* Determine the number of minutes and/or distance for each training zone for that week

— *Step 4:* Select the suitable training protocols to achieve these training goals

— *Step 5:* Record and monitor your plan

When designing a program for young athletes, the coach should follow the following program design methodology. The following figures refer to microcycles for training days throughout the week. Young athletes should follow the "light-hard-light-hard" progression, whilst older and more developed athletes can follow the "light-medium-hard-light" cycle.

Training Phases

For the coach that is training children over the longer term, the year can be divided into 12 months of training. Obviously if the season is shorter, the following principles are applied but over a shorter time period. The first month is the month immediately after the end of the season. Usually the targeted or peak competition concludes the sports season. Therefore, month 12 should be the peak competition, the national championships, the regional championship or the World Championships.

The coach should decide on the peak competition for each athlete and count backwards to establish the number of the relevant months of training. If the national or world championships is the peak competition and it is in September, then October is month one. This program divides the year into six main phases. They are listed below with their relative aims:

Phase	*Aim*	*Month*
Recovery period	Active recovery	Month 1
Early preparation period	General strength and endurance	Months 2 and 3
Preparation period	Maximum strength and general endurance	Months 4 and 5
Pre-competition period	Maximum strength and specific endurance	Months 6 and 7
Early competition period	Specific endurance and sport technique	Months 8 and 9
Peak competition performance	Race/match preparation and peak period	Months 10 through 12

Increasing the load appropriately

Understanding the methods used to increase training load is essential for any coach of young athletes. The amount that children and youths will improve in a particular sport is a direct result of the amount and quality of work they achieve in training. From the early stages of development through to high-performance, athletes must increase their workload in training gradually, according to individual needs.

During the early stages of development it is difficult to monitor training loads, because many increases are the result of normal growth end development. A coach can progressively increase training programs for young developing athletes in the following areas:

— *Duration of sessions:* The length of each training session can increase from the beginning of each season to the end

— *Number of exercises:* Athletes can expand the number of drills and exercises they perform per training session over months and years. An increase in technical drills will lead to significant advances. However as the number of exercises increases the coach must closely monitor the rest intervals between them. Longer rest intervals will give the children more energy to perform all the work for that training session

— *Frequency of training sessions:* To constantly and progressively challenge the bodies of young athletes toward improved performance, you must regularly increase the frequency of training sessions per week. This is essential because skill development occurs during practice and not during competition. For young athletes to master the skills of the sport and develop the motor abilities for future competitions, they must have more training sessions than competitions. There should be a ratio of at least 3 practices to one competition although this ratio should ideally be 4-6 practices per competition

— *Weeks of training:* Extending the season so there are more weeks before the competition period starts will lead to significant improvement in performance. The ideal situation is to practice for most months of the year as this will lead to better development of skills and motor abilities

— *Months of training:* As children become older (16+) and more experienced, they should commit more months to training in a specific sport if they desire high performance results. At first they should increase the duration of training, then the frequency and then the number of exercises.

Working towards a long-term plan

By applying most of the principles and rules that have

been discussed thus far in conjunction with a little common sense, it is not hard to develop a long-term program that takes a young athlete and turns him or her into a successful senior athlete.

The key, however, all revolves around making it fun! As much as you the coach enjoy having fun, so does your young athlete. In fact, if you no longer participate in a sport, this is probably a good opportunity to ask yourself why you no longer compete. The primary answer is probably because you were not enjoying it as much as other aspects of your life. One could even go as far as to say that if you were enjoying your sport to the absolute maximum, you would quite happily sacrifice the time to do it.

The big challenge that you face as the coach is trying to instil exercise and training ethic into the "PlayStation Generation"! Your single biggest challenge as the coach is to make training and participating in sport more fun than the Internet.

How to Prepare for Your Next Competition

This piece was written with road and cross country running in mind but many of the points are relevant to all running disciplines. Races are run with the feet but often won with the head. With two runners of equal ability it is the one who uses his or her head - who focuses, concentrates and thinks best - who comes out on top. And this starts well before the gun goes off.

Tactics

In fact it can start days or weeks before, when coach and athlete discuss and work out race tactics. It even pays to write down the tactics, formulating a race plan for each section of the race and the strategies used to achieve it. The race plan should cover strengths and weaknesses, the way to run each section of the race and alternative plans to deal with unexpected changes. Races rarely go to plan, well, not your plan anyway. There are as many race plans as there are competitors, so you cannot expect it all to go the way coach or athlete wants. Having an alternative strategy allows a quick decision to be made without ground lost as the athlete thinks about what to do next.

Visualisation is also part of the "thinking running" process. If the athlete is familiar with a particular course, have them go over it in their mind in the days before. They imagine their way through the race, picturing the entire course, working out what they might do and feel at various stages. They might also imagine various scenarios, mentally preparing themselves for all eventualities.

Lorraine Moller, New Zealand's last Olympic running medallist, visualised her Barcelona Olympic marathon. She inspected the course exactly 12 months before the race then over the next year ran the race over and over in her mind. The course, the weather, the hills, the stadium layout all held no surprises. She knew what to expect, when to expect it and what her reaction would be. Her visualisation even included picturing herself standing on the medal dais.

Monitoring the Course

The warm up is time get the body ready to race - it is also time to get the mind switched on. This is the time final plans should be made; tactics decided and in cross country and road races, course familiarisation. If possible, the warm up should include a jog over the course or as much of it that can be covered. Most harrier events have a map of the course. Encourage your athletes to familiarise themselves with it.

Have them to take note of the best places to run as they go around on the warm up. For example, it may be better to take a corner wide where the distance may be further but they can run faster or not be caught up in heavy traffic. Note the best ways to approach an obstacle such as a jump or bank. Check where the ground is firm and where the soft muddy patches are. Sometimes going through a puddle gives firmer underfoot conditions than going around it - so get them to check it out before the race. And have them imagine the course with other runners on it. The shortest way could also be the most congested. You do not want them held up by a bottleneck at a jump or narrow track where passing is impossible.

Course knowledge helps set tactics. Knowing there is a downhill coming might allow a runner to surge then get their breath back on the slope. Or a strong uphill runner could put a surge in prior to a hill, confident of ability to maintain the pace while other runners who also surged are wiped out by the climb.

A runner must need to know where they are in relation to the finish. How far to go? How far gone? What lap in a track race? In a harrier event, what landmarks are there to indicate distance to the finish? For instance, the athlete wants to increase pace over the last 400m then start an all out sprint with 100m to go. But it is no good if they do not know where the 400m mark is or the finish line is unsighted around a corner or obscured by the crowd.

Work out these aspects with your athletes while they are getting ready to race. Have them do their thinking and planning before the gun goes off, including possible options should things change. Once the race has started the mind should be on the race - on tactics, the opposition, holding form - not on wondering where they are, which is the best way to go or what is around the corner.

Monitoring oneself

It is important for an athlete to focus on how he or she is running. Good running style and efficiency go together. Is the runner relaxed? Is there good technique? Are they wasting energy? Is tension or bad habits creeping in? If athletes think about how they are running they will run better - if the mind wanders they will start running inefficiently, particularly when fatigue sets in. It is a good idea to teach a 'good form checklist'. The checklist goes head, neck, shoulders, arms, hands, hips, legs. Have athletes ask themselves a series of questions as they run: is my head straight, is my neck relaxed, are my shoulders loose and low, are my elbows at a comfortable, efficient angle, are my hands loose, etc.? If the answer is "yes" go to the next question. If "no" correct it and then go to the next question. The athlete should have: -

— Head looking straight ahead, not up or down

— Jaw not clenched. Watch top runners when there is TV coverage of athletics or cross country, especially when there is a front on shot. Notice the jaw actually flops up and down as the athlete runs

— Neck muscles tension-free

— Shoulders low, not hunched or tense

— Elbows at 90° or greater, not tight

— Arms relaxed and hands swinging through approximately hip height

— Wrists and hands relaxed

— Hips forward, running tall with hips over the centre of gravity

— Strides relaxed without over striding. Over striding is when the foot lands ahead of the centre of gravity which slows the runner down by creating a braking action

— No bouncing in the running action
— Arm action that swings from the shoulder (not from the elbow) in as close to a straight line forward and back as possible. Avoid having the shoulders going side to side and the hands crossing past the mid-point of the chest
— Even if a runner has good running style it's surprising how it goes when tired. Hence the need to keep thinking about style and running form, and employing the checklist as they run

Get runners into the habit of thinking about how they are feeling. Are they pacing themselves well? Can they go faster? Should they go slower? Have them monitor their breathing as it is the best indication of effort.

Athletes need also to think about possible developments. Are they prepared should a rival speed up? If someone did, should your athlete go with them, let them go or catch up gradually? Should they surge to isolate someone else? How can they stay with a group or get onto another group? Do they risk leaving one group and trying to get onto one further ahead and be pulled through to a faster time? We have all seen races where someone loses concentration for a moment and finds themselves 100m or so behind the people they were running with. And at the end of the race are still 100m behind, so they ran the bulk of the race at the same pace as the others but were beaten by 100m. By being aware and staying focussed that gap would not have occurred.

Monitoring the opposition

Thinking must also include opponents in a race. How do opponents react to pace increases? How is their breathing? Have you or your athlete seen any of them before so know their likely tactics? The difference between winning and not winning could come down to knowing how opponents feel, focus, to being switched on. So many things to think about and so many reasons why one cannot afford to let the mind wander. The athlete is the one running the race, he or she is the one who must make the decisions. The coaching process must therefore include training to think.

So how do you train the mind? The same way you train the body - practise. The ideal time to practise concentration is during time trials and rep sessions where there is a need to maintain a specified pace and run efficiently yet not have tactics and opponents to worry about. Low key, preseason or club races are ideal for training the mind, to think about tactics and other race requirements, as well as trying different tactics.

On a training run the mind can wander, thoughts thought, scenery enjoyed and conversations carried on. Not so when racing. That is the time to be a thinking runner.

How to design a session

The circuit training format utilises a group of 6 to 10 strength exercises that are completed one exercise after another. Each exercise is performed for a specified number of repetitions or for a prescribed time period before moving on to the next exercise. The exercises within each circuit are separated by brief, timed rest intervals, and each circuit is separated by a longer rest period. The total number of circuits performed during a training session may vary from two to six depending on your training level, your period of training (preparation or competition) and your training objective.

Identify the possible exercises that can be performed with the available equipment. Identify on paper 3 to 4 circuits of 6 to 10 exercise. In each circuit try to ensure that no two consecutive exercises exercise the same muscle group e.g. do not have press ups followed by pull ups. A circuit should be set up so that you work each body part as follows: Total-body, Upper-body, Lower-body, Core & Trunk etc.

Exercises

The following are examples of exercises that can be used in a circuit training session:

— *Upper-body:* Press ups, Bench dips, Pull ups, Medicine ball chest pass, Bench lift, inclined press up

— *Core & trunk:* Sit ups (lower abdominals), Stomach crunch (upper abdominals), Back extension chest raise

— *Lower-body:* Squat jumps, Compass jumps, Astride jumps, Step ups, Shuttle runs, Hopping shuttles, Bench squat

— *Total-body:* Burpees, Treadmills, Squat thrusts, Skipping

3

Planning for Strength Training

The strength needed for a sprinter to explode from the blocks is different to the strength needed by a weight lifter to lift a 200kg barbell. This therefore implies that there are different types of strength. The classifications of strength are:

— *Maximum strength* - the greatest force that is possible in a single maximum contraction

— *Elastic strength* - the ability to overcome a resistance with a fast contraction

— *Strength endurance* - the ability to express force many times over

A muscle will only strengthen when it is worked beyond its normal operation, it is overloaded. Overload can be progressed by increasing the :

— number of repetitions of an exercise

— number of sets of the exercise

— intensity - reduced recover time

How do we develop each strength ?

— Maximum strength can be developed with :

    — weight training

— Elastic strength can be developed with :

  - — conditioning exercises
  - — complex training sessions
  - — medicine ball exercises
  - — plyometric exercises
  - — weight training
- — Strength endurance can be developed with :
  - — circuit training
  - — dumbbell exercises
  - — weight training
  - — hill and harness running

Weight Training

Better performances can be the product of a number of factors. This product is primarily the outcome of efficient technique, the progression of speed and the maturing competitive attitude on a sound basis of general endurance, all round strength and general mobility. The development of all round strength is best achieved via circuit training and then progressing this through weight training.

How do we get Stronger?

A muscle will only strengthen when forced to operate beyond its customary intensity (overload). Overload can be progressed by increasing the:

- — resistance e.g. adding 10kg to the barbell
- — number of repetitions with a particular weight
- — number of sets of the exercise

Muscle Fibre Hypertrophy

Resistance training will increase the muscle size (hypertrophy). Muscle growth depends on the muscle fibre type activated and the pattern of recruitment. Muscle growth is due to one or more of the following adaptations:

— Increased contractile proteins (actin and myosin)

— Increased number of and size of myofibrils per muscle fibre

— Increased amounts of connective, tendinous and ligamentous tissues

— Increased enzymes and stored nutrients

Which weight training exercises?

The exercise must be specific to the type of strength required, and is therefore related to the particular demands of the event (specificity). The coach should have knowledge of the predominant types of muscular activity associated with the particular event, the movement pattern involved and the type of strength required. Exercises should be identified that will produce the desired development. Although specificity is important, it is necessary in every schedule to include exercises of a general nature - e.g.

— Power Clean

— Power Snatch

— Bench Press

— Back Squats

— Sit Ups

— Deadlift

— Shoulder Press

— Chest Press

— Lat Pull downs

— Lower Back Extensions

— Tricep Press
— Calf Raise
— Bicep Curls
— Leg Curls
— Leg Extension
— Leg Press

These general exercises give a balanced development, and provide a strong base upon which highly specific exercise can be built.

Muscle movement

Muscle contraction is initiated by an electrical charge from the central nervous system. The exercise that causes the greatest amount of electrical activity within the muscle group will potential produce the greatest gains in mass and strength. Lorenzo Cornacchia conducted a series of Electromyographic (EMG) tests to determine which exercises generated a high level of stimulation with in each muscle group. The results were as follows:

Pectoralis Major	Decline dumbbell bench press
Pectoralis Minor	Incline dumbbell bench press
Medial Deltoids	Standing dumbbell side laterals
Posterior Deltoids	Standing dumbbell bent laterals
Anterior deltoids	Standing front dumbbell raises
Biceps Brachii	Incline seated dumbbell curls (alternate)
Triceps Brachii	Triceps press down (angled bar)
Latissimus Dorsi	One arm dumbbell rows (alternate)
Rectus Femoris	Seated leg extensions
Biceps femoris	Standing leg curls

Semitendinosus	Seated leg curls
Gastrocnemius	Standing one leg calf raises

Olympic lifts

The Olympic Lifts are recommended exercises for inclusion in power and speed training programs. The objective of these exercises is to develop the large muscles of the body in an explosive action that requires the use of many joints and muscle groups in a coordinated movement. The Olympic Lifts comprise of the Clean and Jerk and the Snatch. The Power Snatch and Power Clean are auxiliary lifts that aid in the training of the Clean and Jerk and the Snatch.

— Power Clean

— Jerk

— Power Snatch

The amount of weight to be used should be based on a percentage of the maximum amount of weight that can be lifted one time, generally referred to as one repetition maximum (1RM). The maximum number of repetitions performed before fatigue prohibits the completion of an additional repetition is a function of the weight used, referred to as repetition maximum (RM), and reflects the intensity of the exercise. A weight load that produces fatigue on the third repetition is termed a three repetition maximum (3RM) and corresponds to approximately 95% of the weight that could be lifted for 1RM.

For maximum results, athletes should train according to their genetic predisposition. An athlete with a greater proportion of slow twitch muscles would adapt better to endurance training and a muscular endurance program using more repetitions of a lighter weight. An athlete with a greater proportion of fast twitch muscles would benefit from sprint training and a muscular strength program using fewer repetitions of a heavier weight.

Load - repetition relationship

The strength training zone requires you to use loads in the range of 60% to 100% of 1RM. The relationship of percentage loads to number of repetitions (rounded up) to failure is as follows:

— 60% - 17 reps

— 65% - 14 reps

— 70% - 12 reps

— 75% - 10 reps

— 80% - 8 reps

— 85% - 6 reps

— 90% - 5 reps

— 95% - 3 reps

— 100% - 1 rep

The number of repetitions performed to fatigue is an important consideration in designing a strength training program. The greatest strength gains appear to result from working with 4-6RM. Increasing this to 12-20RM favours the increase in muscle endurance and mass.

One set of 4-6RM performed 3 days a week is a typical strength training program. The optimal number of sets of an exercise to develop muscle strength remains controversial. In a number of studies comparing multiple set programs to produce greater strength gains than a single set, the majority of studies indicate that there is not a significant difference.

Handling heavy weights in the pursuit of strength will require a recovery of 3-5 minutes between sets, but only minimum recovery should be taken if strength endurance is the aim. The majority of athletic events are fast and dynamic, and therefore this quality must be reflected in the athlete's strength work. Muscular strength is primarily developed when 8RM or less is used in a set. How much load you use depends upon what it is you wish to develop:

— 1RM to 3RM - neuromuscular strength
— 4RM to 6RM - maximum strength by stimulating muscle hypertrophy
— 6RM to 12RM - muscle size (hypertrophy) with moderate gains in strength
— 12RM to 20RM - muscle size and endurance

Rest Interval between sets

The aim of the recovery period between sets is to replenish the stores of ATP and Creatine Phosphate (CP) in the muscles. An inadequate recovery means more reliance on the Lactic Acid (LA) energy pathway in the next set. Several factors influence the recovery period, including:

— Type of strength you are developing
— The load used in the exercise
— Number of muscle groups used in the exercise
— Your condition
— Your weight

A recovery of three to five minutes or longer will allow almost the complete restoration of ATP/CP.

Rest Interval between sessions

The energy source being used during the training session is probably the most important factor to consider. During the maximum strength phase, when you are primarily using the ATP/CP energy pathway, daily training is possible because ATP/CP restoration is completed within

24 hours. If you are training for muscular endurance (muscle definition) then you require a 48 hour recovery as this is how long it takes to fully restore your glycogen stores.

As a 'rule of thumb' 48 hours should elapse between sessions. If training strenuously, any athlete will find it extremely difficult to maintain the same level of lifting at each session, and the total poundage lifted in each session would be better to be varied (e.g. a high, low and medium volume session) each week.

What sort of weight lifting equipment?

There are variable resistance machines and free weights. Variable resistance machines are effective tools for building strength and muscle tone and are designed to work the target muscle in isolation, without the assistance of the surrounding muscles. Free weights allow you not only to target a particular muscle group but to engage other muscles that assist in the work. Once they are conditioned, these assisting muscles help you to increase the weight you use in training the target muscles in order to stimulate the most growth in muscle fibres. The assisting muscles help stabilise the body, support limbs and maintain posture during a lift. Lifting free weights improves your coordination by improving the neuromuscular pathways that connect your muscles to the central nervous system.

Training Systems

Simple Sets : e.g. 3 x 8 with 70% - meaning three sets of eight repetitions with a weight of 70% of maximum for one repetition. All novice lifters should work on, because the high number of repetitions enables the lifter to learn correct technique, and thereby reduce the risk of injury this system.

Pyramid System : The load is increased and the repetitions are reduced (e.g. 100kg x 10, 120kg x 5, 130kg x 4, 140kg x 3, 150kg x 2, 160kg x 1). Pyramid lifting is only for experienced lifters who have an established good technique.

Super Setting : This consists of performing two or three exercises continuously, without rest in between sets, until all exercises have been performed. The normal 'between sets' rest is taken before the next circuit of exercises is commenced.

Training Programs

Use the above notes to assist you in the preparation of a general strength training program, to develop your general strength, and a specific strength training program to develop your specific strength to meet to the demands of your event/sport.

If weight training facilities is limited to your home and a set of dumbbells then it is still possible to construct a dumbbell weight training program. To monitor progress in training you should conduct strength and muscle balance tests.

Weight Lifting Standards

Weight lifting standards are an indication of the maximum load or one repetition max (1RM) that you should be able to lift for a particular weight lifting exercise based on your gender, body weight and weight lifting experience.

Calculation Parameters

The calculator below, which is appropriate for an adult male in the weight range of 120-320lbs and an adult female in the weight range of 100-200lbs, provides an estimate of the maximum load (1RM) standard for the following weight lifting exercises:

- — Military Press or Shoulder Press
- — Bench Press
- — Squat
- — Deadlift
- — Clean

Three estimates are provided:

1. *Novice* - an adult with less than 1 years experience of regular weight training
2. *Experienced* - an adult with 1 to 2 years experience of regular weight training
3. *Advanced* - an adult with more than 2 years experience of regular weight training

Safety in the weight room

Strength training is safe when properly supervised and controlled. Every weight room should have a set of rules and regulations pertaining to safety and they should be on public display. Rules may vary from one weight room to another but some very basic rules apply to them all:

- — Train only when a qualified coach is present
- — Follow your training schedule
- — Work in pairs - one lifting the other spotting
- — No horseplay
- — Wear the correct clothing and shoes
- — No eating, drinking or smoking
- — No personal stereos with headphones
- — Help and respect other athletes
- — Only athletes who are working out should be in the weight room

Make sure you and your athletes are fully aware of the

safety rules applying to the weight training room(s) you use.

CONDITIONING

One of the misconceptions in the sports world is that a sports person gets in shape by just playing or taking part in his/her chosen sport. If a stationary level of performance, consistent ability in executing a few limited skills is your goal, then engaging only in your sport will keep you there.

However, if you want the utmost efficiency, consistent improvement, and balanced abilities sportsmen and women must participate in year round conditioning programs. The bottom line in sports conditioning and fitness training is stress. Not mental stress, but adaptive body stress. Sportsmen and women must put their bodies under a certain amount of stress to increase physical capabilities.

The components of fitness

Exercise scientists have identified nine components that comprise the definition of fitness. The following lists each of the nine components and an example of how they are used:-

— *Strength* - the extent to which muscles can exert force by contracting against resistance

— *Power* - the ability to exert maximum muscular contraction instantly in an explosive burst of movements

— *Agility* - the ability to perform a series of explosive power movements in rapid succession in opposing directions

— *Balance* - the ability to control the body's position, either stationary (e.g. a handstand) or while moving

(e.g. a gymnastics stunt)

— *Flexibility* - the ability to achieve an extended range of motion without being impeded by excess tissue, i.e. fat or muscle (e.g. executing a leg split)

— *Local Muscle Endurance* - a single muscle's ability to perform sustained work (e.g. rowing or cycling)

— *Cardiovascular Endurance* - the heart's ability to deliver blood to working muscles and their ability to use it (e.g. running long distances)

— *Strength Endurance* - a muscle's ability to perform a maximum contraction time after time (e.g. continuous explosive rebounding through an entire basketball game)

— *Co-ordination-* the ability to integrate the above listed components so that effective movements are achieved.

Of all the nine elements of fitness cardiac respiratory qualities are the most important to develop as they enhance all the other components of the conditioning equation.

Physical fitness

Physical fitness refers to the capacity of an athlete to meet the varied physical demands of their sport without reducing the athlete to a fatigued state. The components of physical fitness are: Strength, Endurance, Speed, Flexibility and Body Composition.

Motor fitness

Motor Fitness refers to the ability of an athlete to perform successfully at their sport. The components of motor fitness are: Agility, Balance, Co-ordination, Power and Reaction Time.

Complex Training

Strength work has been shown to improve sports performance particularly for sprinters, jumpers and throwers but it is not beneficial in developing rate of force - the speed with which force is achieved in a movement. For example, it takes around 400 msec to develop maximum force during a squat exercise, but the foot-ground contact time in sprinting is around 90 msec so there is not enough time to produce maximum force in sprinting. Therefore, for speed strength events, like sprinting, it is the rate of force development that becomes more important than absolute strength.

Rate of force development

To develop the rate of force the Type IIb muscle fibres need to be targeted, as these are ones that produce force most explosively allowing for maximum power. The sorts of exercises that develop the Type IIb fibres are:

— Speed strength exercises e.g. weighted squats jumps

— Plyometric exercises e.g. bounding.

Many athletes include plyometric exercises in their training programs and are well aware of their benefits. However, it is slightly less well known that the combination of traditional strength with power and plyometric exercises together results in greater Type IIb recruitment and consequently greater improvements in power and rate of force development.

What is complex training?

Complex training is a workout comprising of a resistance exercise followed by a matched plyometric exercise e.g.:

— squats followed by squat jumps

— bench press followed by plyometric press up

The logic behind these matched pair of exercises is that the resistance work gets the nervous system in to full action so that more Type IIb fibres are available for the explosive exercise, hence a better training benefit.

Quality not quantity

To get the best from these training workouts you need to be physically fresh and motivated. Type IIb fibres are not magically recruited by just doing the workout, you have to be focused on the exercises and perform them as explosively as possible. Try to avoid hard aerobic or anaerobic sessions for at least 48 hours before a complex session. Once a complex session has started, do not perform any static stretching exercises as this will relax the muscles and reduce force production potential. It is the quality of execution of each exercise that is important, not the quantity. To ensure quality is maintained have the correct rest periods.

Complex training programs

A complex training program can be used in the general, specific and competition phases of training. The following are example workouts for each phase:

General phase

In this phase the athlete should complete all sets of the weights exercise with a recovery of 60 seconds/set. This is followed by a three minute rest before performing all sets of the matched plyometric exercise with a recovery of 90 second/set:

Exercise	*Reps*	*Rest/Set*
Squats	3 × 12RM	60 seconds
Vertical Jumps	3 × 10	90 seconds
Bench Press	3 × 12RM	60 seconds

Medicine ball chest pass	3 × 10	90 seconds
Barbell Lunge	3 × 12RM	60 seconds
Step Jumps	3 × 10	90 seconds
Lat Pull down	3 × 12RM	60 seconds
Medicine ball overhead pass	3 × 10	90 seconds
Abdominal crunches	3 × 20	60 seconds
Medicine ball sit up and throw	3 × 10	90 seconds

Specific phase

The plyometric exercises in the specific phase must be specific to your sport/event. The athlete conducts one set of the weights exercise followed immediately by one set of the Plyometric exercise e.g. 6 squats, 6 drop jumps, 3 minutes rest, 6 squats, 6 drop jumps (with minimal recovery between the squats and drop jumps). 3 × 6 (12RM) means 3 sets of 6 repetitions using a load that would produce 12 repetitions max (RM).

Exercise	*Reps*	*Rest/Set*
SquatsDrop Jumps	3 × 6 (12RM)3 × 6	3 minutes
Barbell step upsHops (each leg)	3 × 6 (12RM)3 × 5	3 minutes
Bench PressPlyometric press up	3 × 6 (12RM)3 × 5	3 minutes
Barbell LungeBox Jumps	3 × 6 (12RM)3 × 10	3 minutes

Competition phase

The plyometric exercises in the competition phase must be specific to your sport/event. As in the specific phase of training, the athlete conducts one set of the weights exercise followed immediately by one set of the plyometric exercise. 2 × 4 (8RM) means 2 sets of 4 repetitions using a load that would produce 8 repetitions max (RM).

Exercise	*Reps*	*Rest/Set*

SquatsHops (each leg)	2 × 4 (8RM)2 × 6	5 minutes
Bench PressPlyo press up	2 × 4 (8RM)2 × 5	5 minutes
Barbell LungeSpeed bounds	2 × 4 (8RM)2 × 10	5 minutes

Training program for speed improvement

The following program was devised by Barry Ross a USA track and field coach with 25 years experience to increase the running speed of his athletes. Speed is considered to be the combination of two factors - stride rate and stride length. Greater forces increase the stride length and decrease the contact time so stride rate increases. To improve these factors coaches have focused on developing leg strength that in turn has resulted in an increase in body weight. What we ideally require in our runner is a high power to weight ratio. The objective of Barry's program is to increase strength with minimal gain in bulk thereby achieving a high power to weight ratio.

1. Warm up and dynamic stretching
2. Deadlift - 2 to 3 sets of 2 to 3 reps @ 85 to 95% 1RM - each set followed by 6 depth jumps and then a 5 minute recovery
3. Bench Press - 2 to 3 sets of 2 to 3 reps @ 85 to 95% 1RM with a 5 minute recovery between each set
4. Power Clean - 2 to 3 sets of 2 to 3 reps @ 85 to 95% 1RM with a 5 minute recovery between each set
5. Abdominal exercises - 3 to 5 sets of 3 to 5 reps @ 85 to 95% 1RM with a 5 minute recovery between each set
6. Cool down and static stretching

Medicine Ball

The ability to generate strength and power is a very important component for success in many sports, particularly in those involving explosive movements.

Medicine ball training, in conjunction with a program of weight training and circuit training, can be used to develop strength and power. Certain medicine ball exercises can also be used as part of a plyometric training program to develop explosive movements. Medicine ball training is appropriate to all levels of ability, age, development and sport. To be most effective the program should contain exercises that match the pattern of movements of the sport.

Planning a program

The following are some guidelines in planning and running a medicine ball session:

— Always ensure the athletes carry out a thorough warm up and cool down

— Before starting a session, explain the procedures for each exercise with your athletes

— Partners who feed the medicine ball on certain exercises should be well drilled on what is required

— Medicine ball exercises must precede high intensity work

— Start sessions with lighter less dynamic exercises, then progress to heavier exercises

— The program should have exercises that match the pattern of movements of the sport

— Plan the program to exercise alternate body parts (legs, upper body, torso)

— You will need to have a number of different weights of ball available - heavy, medium and light

— Initially, athletes should use a light weight ball and gradually progress to heavier ones

— Check there is sufficient space (including ceiling height) and that the structure of the walls are safe if any rebounding exercises are used

- Maintain good discipline as medicine balls can be dangerous if used incorrectly
- An effective work-out with medicine balls can be achieved in about 30 to 40 minutes, if the athlete works efficiently
- Quality of movement is more beneficial than quantity of exercise repetitions or sets

Technique and safety

To ensure personal safety and good technique while doing medicine ball exercises the following points should be remembered:

- Complete throws with full extension of the arms
- On standing exercises plant feet before beginning to throw the ball
- Always use the full joint range in the correct sequence in carrying out each exercise
- Maintain technique - do not sacrifice control for distance
- Inexperienced athletes should not take the ball too far back behind the head when carrying out overhead throws
- When picking a ball, ensure the knees are bent and the back is kept straight
- When carrying out exercises lying on your back, ensure the lower back always remains in contact with the surface
- Prior to a catch, ensure you:
  - keep arms extended
  - keep hands together
  - keep eyes on the ball

— reach out to meet the ball prior to making contact

— do not attempt to catch balls thrown wildly

The following is an example of a program of general medicine ball exercises.

Standing torso twist

— Stand back to back 1 metre apart

— Keep your hips facing forward and legs slightly relaxed

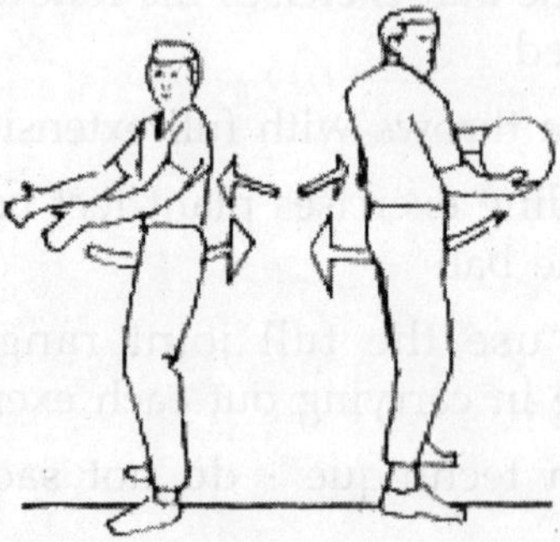

— Pass the ball to one another by only twisting the torso

How many - Two sets of ten reps

Hamstring curls

— Lie flat on the ground

— Roll the ball along the back of legs

— On reaching the heels the ball is flicked up.

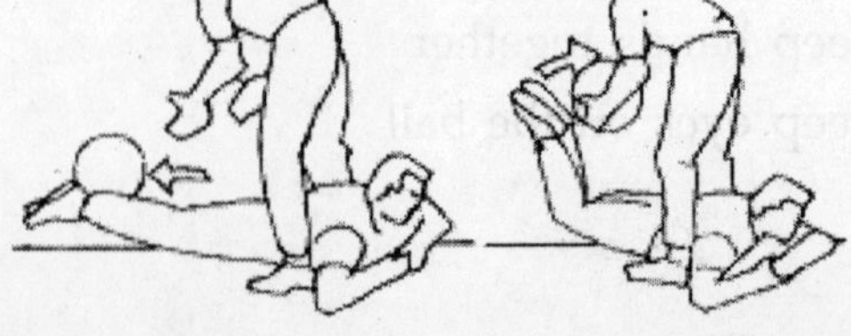

How many - Two sets of eight reps

Chest push

— Feet together.

— Hands behind ball and elbows out.

— Step forward and push ball upwards and towards your partner.

How many - Two sets of eight reps

Vertical extensions

— Stand back to back approx. 60cm apart

— Ball is passed overhead

— Ball is returned between the knees

How many - One set of ten reps

Lay back double arm throw

— Support your back with a large medicine ball

— Throw another medicine ball to your partner

— Partner returns ball to an overhead position

How many - Two sets of eight reps

Double leg kicks

— Lie on your back

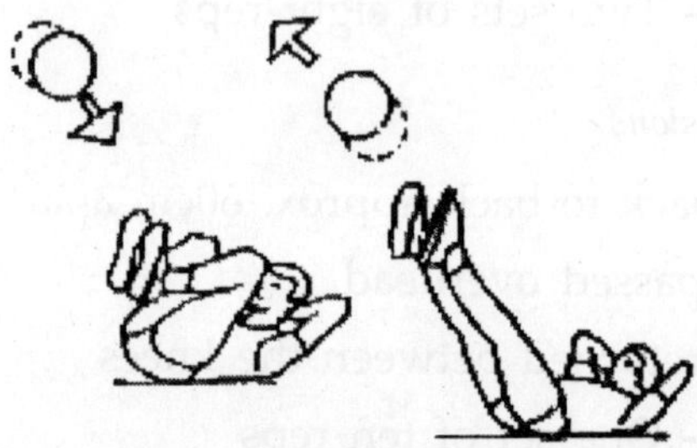

— Soles of feet facing partner · Partner stands 3 metres away.

— Partner throws ball in a looping path onto your feet.

— Bending your knees back to your chest the ball is then kicked back to your partner.

— Do not lower your legs to the ground.

How many - Two sets of ten reps.

Straight arm standing throw

— Place one foot 50 cm behind the other.

— Take the ball back, ensure hands are high, shoulders stretched and chest out.

— Step forward and throw the ball to your partner, keeping the arms straight.

How many - Two sets of eight reps

Abdominal curl

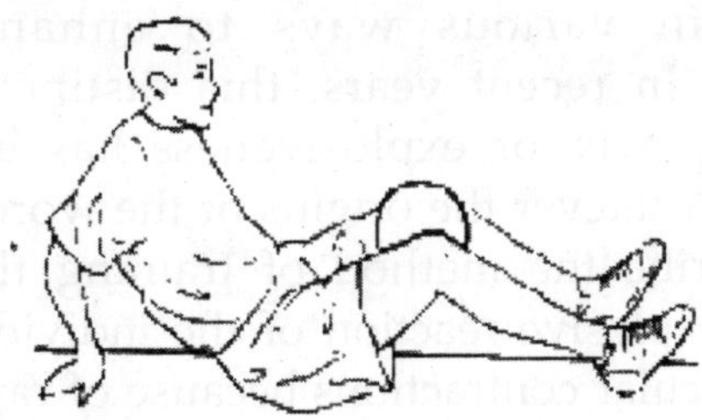

— Sitting up slightly, resting on your hands

— Knees bent

— Ball is held by the knees

— Draw knees up to the chest

— Return to the starting position

How many - One set of twelve reps.

An effective workout with medicine balls can be achieved in about 30 to 40 minutes, if the athlete works efficiently. Carry out two or three sessions per week with a recovery period of 36 to 48 hours between sessions. Each session should be made up of 8 to 10 exercises with the athlete performing 2 to 3 sets of each exercise. If the athlete is to develop strength and muscular endurance then conduct 6 to 12 repetitions (reps) of each exercise. If the athlete is to develop muscular endurance rather than strength then conduct 12 to 30 repetitions. The weight of medicine ball - 3Kg for boys and 2Kg for girls.

Plyometrics

Speed and strength are integral components of fitness found in varying degrees in virtually all athletic movements. Simply put the combination of speed and strength is power. For many years, coaches and athletes have sought to improve power in order to enhance performance. Throughout this century and no doubt long before, jumping, bounding and hopping exercises have been used in various ways to enhance athletic performance. In recent years, this distinct method of training for power or explosiveness has been termed plyometrics. Whatever the origins of the word the term is used to describe the method of training that seeks to enhance the explosive reaction of the individual through powerful muscular contractions because of rapid eccentric contractions.

Muscle mechanism

The maximum force that a muscle can develop is attained during a rapid eccentric contraction. However, it should be realised that muscles seldom perform one type of contraction in isolation during athletic movements. When a concentric contraction occurs (muscle shortens) immediately following an eccentric contraction (muscle lengthens) then the force generated can be dramatically increased.

If a muscle is stretched, much of the energy required to stretch it is lost as heat, but some of this energy can be stored by the elastic components of the muscle. This stored energy is available to the muscle only during a subsequent contraction. It is important to realise that this energy boost is lost if the eccentric Contraction is not followed immediately by a concentric contraction. To express this greater force the muscle must contract within the shortest time possible. This whole process is frequently called the stretch shortening cycle and is the underlying mechanism of plyometric training.

Choose the method to fit the sport

The golden rule of any conditioning program is specificity. This means that the movement you perform in training should match, as closely as possible, the movements encountered during competition. If you are rugby player, practising for the lineout or a volleyball player interested in increasing vertical jump height, then drop jumping or box jumping may be the right exercise. However if you are a javelin thrower aiming for a more explosive launch, then upper body plyometrics is far more appropriate.

Plyometric exercises

The following are examples of lower body and upper body plyometric exercises.

Lower body

Drop jumping

This exercise involves the athlete dropping (not jumping) to the ground from a raised platform or box, and then immediately jumping up. The drop down gives the pre-stretch to the leg muscles and the vigorous drive upwards the secondary concentric contraction. The exercise will be more effective the shorter the time the feet are in contact with the ground. The loading in this exercise is governed by the height of the drop that should be in the region of 30 to 80 cm. Drop jumping is a relatively high impact form of plyometric training and would normally be introduced after the athlete had become accustomed to lower impact alternatives, such as two-footed jumping on the spot.

Bounding and hurdling

If forward motion is more the name of your game, try some bounding. This is a form of plyometric training, where over sized strides are used in the running action and extra time spent in the air. Two-legged bounds reduce the impact to be endured, but to increase the intensity one legged bounding, or hopping, can be used. Bounding upstairs is a useful way to work on both the vertical and horizontal aspects of the running action. Multiple jumps over a series of obstacles like hurdles are valuable drills for athletes training for sprinting or jumping events.

Examples of lower body plyometric exercises with intensity level:

— Standing based jumps performed on the spot (low intensity) - Tuck Jumps, Split Jumps

— Jumps from standing (low-medium intensity) - Standing long jump, Standing hop, standing jump for height

— Multiple jumps from standing (medium intensity) - bounds, bunny hops, double footed jumps over low hurdle, double footed jumps up steps

— Multiple jumps with run in (High intensity) - 11 stride run + 2 hops and a jump into sandpit, 2 stride run in + bounds

— Depth jumping (high-very high intensity) - jumps down and up off box (40 to 100cm), bounding up hill

— Eccentric drop and hold drills (high-very high intensity) - hop and hold, bound/hop/bound/hop over 30 metres (athletes stop and hold on each landing before springing into the next move), drop and hold from a height greater than one metre

Upper body

A variety of drills can be used to make the upper body more explosive:

— *Press ups and hand clap:* Press-ups with a hand clap in between is a particularly vigorous way to condition the arms and chest. The pre-stretch takes place as the hands arrive back on the ground and the chest sinks, and this is followed quickly by the explosive upwards action. Once again, to get the best training effect keep the time in contact with the ground to a minimum.

— *Medicine ball:* Another means of increasing upper body strength popular with throwers is to lie on the ground face up. A partner then drops a medicine ball down towards the chest of the athlete, who catches the ball (pre-stretch) and immediately throws it back. This is another high-intensity exercise and should only be used after some basic conditioning.

Planning a plyometric session

The choice of exercises within a session and their order should be planned. A session could:

— begin with exercises that are fast, explosive and designed for developing elastic strength (low hurdle jumps; low drop jumps)

— work through exercises that develop concentric strength (standing long jump; high hurdle jumps)

— finish with training for eccentric strength (higher drop jumps)

An alternative session could be:

— begin with low hurdle jumps

— progress to bounding and hopping,

— continue with steps or box work

— finish with medicine ball work out for abdominals and upper body

Warm up

A thorough warm up is essential prior to plyometric training. Attention should be given to jogging, stretching (static and ballistic), striding and general mobility especially about the joints involved in the planned plyometric session. A cool down should follow each session.

How many?

It is wise not to perform too many repetitions in any one session and since it is a quality session, with the emphasis on speed and power rather than endurance, split the work into sets with ample recovery in between. An experienced athlete conducting lower body plyometrics may conduct up to 150-200 contacts in a session - athletes new to plyometric work should start with around 40 contacts per session e.g. 3 sets of 10 bunny hops is 30 contacts. Similar approach should be taken with upper body plyometrics.

Where to do it and what to wear

For bounding exercises use surfaces such as grass or resilient surfaces. Avoid cement floors because there is no cushioning. Choose well-cushioned shoes that are stable and can absorb some of the inevitable impact. All athletes should undergo general orthopaedic screening before engaging in plyometric training. Particular attention should be given to structural or postural problems that are likely to predispose the athlete to injury.

Conditioning for plyometrics

Higher than normal forces are put on the musculoskeletal system during plyometric exercises so it is important for the athlete to have a good sound base of general strength and endurance. Most experts state that a thorough grounding in weight training is essential before you start plyometrics. It has been suggested that an athlete be able to squat twice his body weight before attempting depth jumps. However, less intensive plyometric exercises can be incorporated into general circuit and weight training during the early stages of training to progressively condition the athlete. Simple plyometric drills such as skipping hopping and bounding should be introduced first. More demanding exercises such as flying start single-leg hops and depth jumps should be limited to thoroughly conditioned athletes.

Young athletes

Some authors suggest that moderate jumps can be included in the athletic training of very young children. However, great care needs to be exerted when prescribing any training procedures for preadolescent children. Because of the relatively immature bone structure in preadolescent and adolescent children the very great forces exerted during intensive depth jumps should be avoided.

Circuit Training

Circuit training is an excellent way to improve mobility, strength and stamina. The circuit training format utilises a group of 6 to 10 strength exercises that are completed one exercise after another. Each exercise is performed for a specified number of repetitions or for a prescribed time before moving on to the next exercise. The exercises within each circuit are separated by brief, timed rest intervals, and each circuit is separated by a longer rest period. The total number of circuits performed during a training session may vary from two to six depending on your training level (beginner, intermediate, or advanced), your period of training (preparation or competition) and your training objective.

Planning

Identify the possible exercises that can be performed with the available equipment. Identify on paper 3 to 4 circuits of 6 to 10 exercise. In each circuit try to ensure that no two consecutive exercises exercise the same muscle group. e.g. do not have press ups followed by pull ups. A circuit should be set up so that you work each body part as follows: Total-body, Upper-body, Lower-body, Core and Trunk etc.For each circuit I have a set of linoleum cards (6 inches by 6 inches) with an exercise written on each that I lay by the equipment to indicate to the athletes the required exercise at each stage of the circuit. It is important to warm up with easy jogging and stretching exercises and to repeat this as a cool down after the session. The following are examples of exercises that can be used in a circuit training session:

— Upper-body
    — Press ups, Bench dips, Pull ups, Medicine ball chest pass, Bench lift, Inclined press up

- Core and trunk
  - Sit ups (lower abdominals), Stomach crunch (upper abdominals), Back extension chest raise
- Lower-body
  - Squat jumps, Compass jumps, Astride jumps, Step ups, Shuttle runs, Hopping shuttles, Bench squat
- Total-body
  - Burpees, Treadmills, Squat thrusts, Skipping

Example Circuit Training Sessions

6 Exercises

- Treadmills, Press ups, Squat Jumps (forward astride), Sit ups (bent knees feet on the ground), Squat Thrusts, Bench Dips

8 Exercises

- Treadmills, Press ups, Squat Jumps (forward astride), Sit ups (bent knees feet on the ground), Squat Thrusts, Bench Dips, Shuttle runs, Back extension chest raise

Duration

- 20 to 30 seconds work on each exercise with a 30 second recovery between each exercise
- 3 to 5 sets with a 3 minute recovery between each set

The duration can be based on time (e.g. 30 seconds) or set to half the number of repetitions of the exercise the athlete can complete in 60 seconds of 100% effort.

If training is based on the number of repetitions then regular testing (e.g. every 4 weeks) will need to be carried out to determine the maximum number of repetitions that can be completed in 60 seconds for each exercise.

Training can be based on a four week cycle comprising of an easy week, medium week, hard week and test/recovery week. The workload can be varied by changing the number of exercises, duration, sets or repetitions.

Example basic program

Identify a circuit of 8 exercises so that you work each body part as follows: Total-body, Upper-body, Lower-body, Core and Trunk, Total-body, Upper-body, Lower-body, Core and Trunk

	Exercise		*Circuits*	
Week	*Work*	*Rest*	*Number*	*Rest*
1	20 sec	20 sec	2	2 min
2	30 sec	30 sec	2	2 min
3	40 sec	40 sec	2	3 min
4	20 sec	20 sec	3	2 min
5	30 sec	30 sec	3	2 min
6	30 sec	30 sec	4	2 min
7	40 sec	40 sec	3	3 min
8	30 sec	30 sec	3	2 min

Complete the circuit training session twice a week with at least 48 hours between each session. If you are carrying out other training on the same day then the circuit session should follow, with a suitable recovery period, the other session.

Advantages and disadvantages

Advantages of circuit training are:

— Develops strength and endurance
— Appropriate form of training for most sports

— Can be adjusted to suit age, fitness and health of the athlete

— Exercises are simple enough to make each athlete feel a sense of achievement in completing them

— A wide range of exercises to select from which will maintain the athlete's enthusiasm

Disadvantages of circuit training are:

— Many exercises require specialised equipment - e.g. gym equipment

— Ample space required to set up the circuit exercises and equipment

— In general can only be conducted where appropriate facilities/equipment are available

— Use of additional equipment requires appropriate health and safety monitoring

Stage training

In stage training, the required number of repetitions and sets are performed for each exercise before moving to the next exercise. A rest is allowed between each set (e.g. 30 seconds). The number of repetitions can be based on time (e.g. 20 seconds) or set to one third of the number the athlete can complete in 60 seconds of 100% effort. The number of sets - five to eight.

A 5k Circuit

Warm up with two miles of easy running, follow with some stretching routines and then perform the following activities in order. Move quickly from exercise to exercise, but do not perform the exercises themselves too quickly.

1. Run 4 x 100 metres at close to top speed, with short recoveries

2. Run 200 metres (or ¼ mile) at 5k race pace
3. Complete 20 squat thrusts with jumps (burpees).
4. Do 15 "side sit ups" on your left side and then 15 on your right. To complete a side sit up, lie on your left side with your left leg flexed at the knee and lying under your right leg, which is straight. Let the left side of your upper torso lie relaxed on the ground, and fold your arms over the front of your trunk. Then, slowly raise your torso with a twisting motion so that you end up with your torso upright and perpendicular to the ground, and your chest and face facing forward. Slowly lower your upper torso back to the starting position on the ground to complete one rep. Complete 15 sit ups with your left side down and then shift over to the right for 15 more.
5. Perform 20 lunges with each leg. Do each lunge from a six inch platform or step, so that the forward, lunging foot undergoes an exaggerated downward acceleration.
6. Run 400 metres at 5k pace.
7. Do 15 feet elevated press ups.
8. Complete 15 one leg squats with your right leg and then 15 more with your left
9. Perform 30 low back extensions with a twisting motion (i.e., instead of lifting your upper body straight up as you lie flat on the ground with your belly touching earth, your arms at your sides, and your palms on the ground, lift and twist your upper body to the right during the first rep, lift and twist your torso to the left during the second, to the right during the third, etc. Naturally, you will need to untwist your upper body each time your trunk moves back toward the ground so that your stomach

and chest, not your sides, touch the ground. Always do this rhythmically and smoothly, while maintaining good control.

10. Run 400 metres at 5k pace.
11. Carry out 20 bench dips.
12. Hop on your right foot, covering 20 metres as fast as you can; then do the same on your left foot.
13. Complete 15 high bench step ups with each leg.
14. Run 1600 metres at 5k pace
15. Repeat steps 3 to 14 one more time (for two circuits in all), and then cool down with 2 miles of light jogging

Half marathon circuit

Warm up with two miles of easy running, follow with some stretching routines and then perform the following activities in order. Move quickly from exercise to exercise, but don't perform the exercises themselves too quickly.

1. 5 x 100 metres at close to top speed, with short recoveries
2. Run one mile at your goal half-marathon velocity
3. Complete 20 squat thrusts with jumps (burpees)
4. Do 70 abdominal crunches
5. Perform 20 lunges with each leg, with your non lunging foot on a step or platform which is about six inches off the ground.
6. Carry out 70 low back extensions
7. Do 20 press-ups
8. Complete 15 one leg squats with your right leg and then 15 more with your left
9. Run one mile at goal half marathon velocity

10. Carry out 30 bench dips
11. Complete 15 high bench step ups with each leg
12. Jump 100 times in place, getting your propulsive force from your ankles, not your knees, and carrying out the last 30 jumps at an especially quick tempo.
13. Carry out 30 cross body leg swings with each leg. To do these, lean slightly forward with your hands on a wall (or other support) and your full body weight on your left leg. Then, swing your right leg to the left in front of your body, pointing your toes upward as your foot reaches its farthest point of motion. After this, swing your right leg back to the right as far as comfortably possible, again pointing your toes up as your foot reaches it final point of movement. Repeat this overall motion 30 times before performing 30 reps with your left leg .
14. Run one mile at goal half-marathon velocity.
15. Repeat steps 3 to 14 one more time, and then cool down with two miles of light jogging.

Marathon circuit

Warm up with two miles of easy running,d follow with some stretching routines and then perform the following activities in order. Move quickly from exercise to exercise, but don't perform the exercises themselves too quickly.

1. Run 800 metres at what feels like 10K intensity
2. Complete 15 burpees (squat thrusts with jumps)
3. Perform 12 press ups
4. Do 12 one leg squats with each leg
5. Run 800 metres at a little faster than marathon speed
6. Carry out 50 abdominal crunches
7. Complete 12 lunges with each leg

8. Perform 50 low back extensions
9. Run 800 metres at a little faster than goal marathon speed
10. Do 12 feet elevated press ups
11. Do 15 bench dips
12. Carry out 12 high bench step ups
13. Run 1600 metres at a little faster than goal marathon speed
14. Repeat steps 2 to 13 twice more (for three circuits in all)
15. Cool down with two miles of easy running

These circuits build a tremendous foundation of whole body strength and fatigue resistance, both of which are critically important for marathon running. The circuits also improve efficiency while running at marathon intensity and help to raise lactate threshold. Finally, the marathon circuits enhance your ability to run at goal marathon tempo when you are very tired, and they are a tremendous confidence builder.

Dumbbell Exercises

The various exercises that can be performed using dumbbells.

Exercises

Decline dumbbell bench press

Muscles - Pectoralis Major (lower chest), Anterior Deltoids

— Grasp two dumbbells using an overhand grip while sitting at the high end of a decline bench

— Rest the dumbbells in an upright position on the knees

— Lie on the flat bench, simultaneously bringing the dumbbells to a position where they are held at the sides of the torso at chest level

— Raise the dumbbells to a position of straight arm's length (elbows not locked)

— At this point, the dumbbells are held directly over the chest area, in contact with each other, with palms facing forward

— Slowly bend the arms and lower the dumbbells until they are at either side of the chest

— Dumbbells are lowered to a position where a comfortable but maximum stretch is achieved

— Raise the dumbbells from the sides of the chest to the starting position

Incline dumbbell bench press

Muscles - Pectoralis Minor (upper chest), Anterior Deltoids

— Grasp the dumbbells using an overhand grip while sitting at the edge of the incline bench

— Rest the dumbbells in an upright position on the knees

— Lie on the incline bench, simultaneously bringing the dumbbells to a position where they are held at the sides of the torso at chest level

— Raise the dumbbells to a position of straight arm's length (elbows not locked)

— At this point, the dumbbells are held directly over the upper chest, in contact with each other, while the palms are facing forward

— Slowly bend the arms and lower the dumbbells until they are at either side of the chest

— Dumbbells are lowered to a position where a comfortable stretch is achieved
— Raise the dumbbells from the sides of the chest to the starting position.

Standing dumbbell side laterals

Muscles - Medial Deltoids

— Stand with back straight, knees slightly bent, and feet slightly less than shoulder-width apart
— Keep back erect and elbows slightly flexed throughout the entire movement
— Grasp the dumbbells using an overhand grip, with palms facing each other
— Press dumbbells together approximately 4 to 6 inches in front of the hips
— Keeping elbows slightly bent, raise the dumbbells laterally, in an arc toward the ceiling until arms are parallel to the floor, and hold briefly
— Slowly lower the dumbbells to the starting position

Standing dumbbell bent laterals

Muscles - Posterior Deltoids, Medial Deltoids, upper Trapezius

— Stand with back straight, knees bent, and feet shoulder-width apart
— Grasp the dumbbells using an overhand grip, with palms facing each other
— Bend at the hips until back is parallel to the floor and arms are hanging down in an extended position (arms perpendicular to the floor)
— Keeping elbows slightly bent, raise the dumbbells laterally in an arc-like motion until arms are parallel to the floor

— Slowly lower the dumbbells to the starting position.

Standing front dumbbell raises (alternate)

Muscles - Anterior deltoids

— Stand with back straight, knees slightly bent, and feet slightly less than shoulder-width apart

— Grasp the dumbbells using an overhand grip with palms facing downward

— Let arms hang straight down at the sides, holding the dumbbells approximately 2 to 4 inches from upper thigh level

— Keeping elbows slightly bent throughout the entire movement, raise the left dumbbell from upper thigh level to eye level, and slowly lower dumbbell to starting position

— Repeat the movement with the right dumbbell.

Incline seated dumbbell curls (alternate)

Muscles - Biceps Brachii

— Lie on an incline bench with back pressed firmly against the padding and feet flat on the floor

— Hang arms down at the sides, holding the dumbbells with an underhand grip (palms facing upward)

— Slowly curl the left dumbbell toward your left shoulder

— When maximum biceps contraction occurs, slowly lower the dumbbell to the starting position

— Repeat with the right arm

Seated one arm triceps extension

Muscles - Triceps Brachii

— Sit on a flat bench with feet flat on the floor

— Grasp a dumbbell with an overhand grip (palms are facing forward throughout the entire movement)
— Hold the dumbbell overhead with the arm fully extended
— Lower the dumbbell until the forearm is parallel to the floor
— At this point, the dumbbell is positioned behind the neck (end position)
— Without bouncing the weight at the bottom of the movement, slowly extend the dumbbell to the starting position and repeat the movement until the desired number of repetitions is completed
— Repeat for the other hand.

One arm dumbbell rows (alternate)

Muscles - Latissimus Dorsi, Biceps, Brachialis, Trapezius (mid)

— Grasp a dumbbell with the right hand, using an overhand grip (palm facing the body)
— Rest the left knee on a flat bench. Right leg should be flexed with the foot flat on the floor
— Bend forward at the hips and stabilise the body with a straightened left arm
— At this point, the torso should be nearly parallel to the floor
— The dumbbell in the right hand is held at full arm's length
— Keeping the elbow close to the torso, pull the dumbbell upward in a straight vertical line, allowing it to lightly touch the rib cage
— Slowly lower the dumbbell to the starting position, and repeat the movement until the desired number of repetitions is completed
— Repeat for the left hand.

Lunges with dumbbells

Muscles - Quadriceps, Hamstrings, Gluteal muscles

— Grasp a dumbbell with each hand
— Hold the dumbbells at the .sides of the body with arms fully extended (palms facing your torso)
— Step forward with the lead leg (stepping leg), keeping the back erect
— Bend the knee of lead leg until it has reached a 90 degree angle
— At this point, the knee of the back leg should be approximately 2 to 3 inches from the floor
— When fully lowered, push forcefully with the lead leg and return to the starting position
— Repeat the exercise with your other leg, and continue to alternate until the desired number of repetitions is completed
— Remember that a shorter lead step allows more emphasis to be placed on the quadriceps muscles and a larger step places more emphasis on the gluteal and hamstring muscles.

Squats

Muscles - Rectus Femoris

— Grasp the dumbbells with an underhand grip (palms facing the torso)
— Stand with back erect, knees slightly bent, and feet shoulder width apart
— Arms fully extend at the side of the body
— Lower the body until the thighs are parallel with the ground
— Straighten the legs to return to the start position.

Wrist Curls

Muscles - Forearm flexors

— Grasp a dumbbell with an underhand grip (palm facing upward)

— Sit on the end of a bench, feet flat on the floor

— Allow the forearm to lie on the thigh with the wrist and hand hanging over the end of the knee

— Allow the dumbbell to be lowered until it is rolled into the fingers

— Using the forearm muscles raise the dumbbell by flexing the fingers and curling the wrist

— Lower the weight to the start position

— Repeat for required number of repetitions

— Repeat with the other hand.

Wrist extensions

Muscles - Forearm flexors

— Grasp a dumbbell with an overhand grip (palm facing downward)

— Sit on the end of a bench, feet flat on the floor

— Allow the forearm to lie on the thigh with the wrist and hand hanging over the end of the knee

— Allow the dumbbell to be lowered until it is rolled into the fingers

— Using the forearm muscles raise the dumbbell by curling the wrist

— Lower the weight to the start position

— Repeat for required number of repetitions

— Repeat with the other hand.

Hill Training

Hill running has a strengthening effect as well as boosting your athlete's power and is ideal for those athletes who depend on high running speeds - football, rugby, basketball, cricket players and even runners. To reduce the possibility of injury hill training should be conducted once the athlete has a good solid base of strength and endurance.

What it does for you

In hill running, the athlete is using their body weight as a resistance to push against, so the driving muscles from which their leg power is derived have to work harder. The technique to aim for is a "bouncy" style where the athlete has a good knee lift and maximum range of movement in the ankle. They should aim to drive hard, pushing upwards with their toes, flexing their ankle as much as possible, landing on the front part of the foot and then letting the heel come down below the level of the toes as the weight is taken.

This stretches the calf muscles upwards and downwards as much as possible and applies resistance which overtime will improve their power and elasticity. The athlete should look straight ahead, as they run (not at their feet) and ensure their neck, shoulders and arms are free of tension. Many experts believe that the "bouncy" action is more important than the speed at which the athlete runs up the hills.

Hill work results in the calf muscles learning to contract more quickly and thereby generating work at a higher rate, they become more powerful. The calf muscle achieves this by recruiting more muscle fibres, around two or three times as many when compared to running on the flat. The "bouncy" action also improves the power of the quads in the front of the thigh as they provide the high knee lift that is required. For the athlete, when competing in their sport/event, it can mean higher running speeds and shorter foot strike times. Hill training offers the following benefits:

— helps develop power and muscle elasticity
— improves stride frequency and length
— develops co-ordination, encouraging the proper use of arm action during the driving phase and feet in the support phase
— develops control and stabilisation as well as improved speed (downhill running)
— promotes strength endurance
— develops maximum speed and strength (short hills)
— improves lactate tolerance (mixed hills)

The benefits of short, medium and long hills are quite different, and can be used at different times of the year.

Short hills

A short hill is one which takes no more that 30 seconds to run up and has an inclination between 5 and 15 degrees gradient. The athlete's energy source on short hills is entirely anaerobic. The athlete should focus on a running technique which has vigorous arm drive and high knee lift, with the hips kept high, so that they are 'running tall', not leaning forwards.

The session is anaerobic so the recovery time can be long, a walk back down the hill, or a slow jog of 60 to 90 seconds. The total volume will depend on the fitness of the athlete and the reason for doing it. A sprinter looking for strength might do 10 repetitions of 15 second duration up a steep slope with a long recovery where as a distance runner who is trying to improve sprinting speed might do 30 repetitions of 15 seconds duration.

Short hills of 5 to 10 second duration will help improve the Adenosine Triphosphate and Phosphate-creatine (ATP+PC) energy system and hills of 15 to 30 second duration will help develop the ATP+PC+muscle glycogen energy system. Example of short hill sessions:

— 8 to 10 repetitions over 50 metres (sprinters and hurdlers)

— 8 to 10 repetitions over 40 metres (jumpers and throwers)

— 8 to 10 repetitions over 150 metres (middle distance athletes)

— 8 to 10 repetitions over 200 metres (long distance athletes)

Long hills

A long hill is one which takes from 90 seconds to three minutes plus. Here most of the energy comes from aerobic sources, but if parts of the hill are steep and they are running them hard, there will still be an accumulation of blood lactate. There will be local muscular fatigue in the leg muscles, and possibly in the abdominal muscles too, but the main limiting factor will be the athlete's cardiovascular system. These hills can be used in two ways:

— as a hard aerobic training session during the pre-competition season

— as a hard time-trial session in the early part of the competition period.

As these hill sessions are aerobic, the athlete will not use as much power per stride as the shorter hills, and so perhaps would not be used by middle-distance runners, except for one or two time-trial runs. They are particularly good for the cross country or road runner who is running distances of 10,000m and upwards. A session of, say eight three minutes, with a run back of four or five minutes will make a good hard workout.

Mixed hill running

The attraction of mixed hill training is that it can be fitted in with the terrain the athlete is running on and can, therefore, be interesting and full of variety. If they do a fartlek session round a hilly course, they will be able to fit in a number of different runs. Two advantages can come from this type of hill training:

— *Race simulation.* It is a good principle to rehearse in training the situations they are likely to meet in a race, such as trying to break open a gap by running hard over the top of a hill and keeping the pace going instead of easing up, as many runners do.

— *Downhill running.* This is something that often causes jarring and strains.

Mixed hill running can also be used to improve running economy and boost an athlete's VO2 max. To do this identify a six or seven mile undulating hilly course, commence the session jogging at a modest pace and gradually pick up the intensity as they move through the hills. The key is not just to run up and down a few hills in their workout but to find a place where they can run up and down hills nearly constantly. If they cannot find a six or seven mile course with constant undulations, use a shorter course and run back and forth on it. The key is not to let the flat ground running total more than 25% of the workout.

During most of the run, the athlete's heart rate should be close to 85% of maximum (85% of maximum heart rate matches up with 76% VO2 max). Do not let them blast up hills in the early part of the workout, this can stop them working though subsequent miles. The idea is to run constantly at a hard but not super fast speed. They should not feel like they are racing but as though they are running just slightly slower than lactate threshold, even if the actual pace is even slower than that. Alternatively, they can use heart rate, which should be at around 85% of maximum during at least the last two-thirds of their run. A run of six to seven miles in this manner is enough for a great workout, but you can expand the session as much as you want with some additional hilly, but easier miles. If you plan in a mixed hill session once a week over 10 to 12 mile course, you will be amazed at how their running takes off.

Rough terrain

There are many advantages of combining hills and hard going e.g. sand. When the sand is soft, the athlete has to work a lot harder, and increase their leg speed to keep themselves going. At the same time, there is a reduced risk of damaging their legs through impact injuries. In general, it has the same effect as hill running, but the distances can be reduced because of the difficulty. Other methods of building leg strength are running in boots, running through snow or running with a pack on your back. As the coach remember, the tougher the session the more carefully it must be integrated into the overall training plan.

Planning in the hill training

Once an athlete is fit enough to train, hill running can form a regular part of the pre-competition build-up. To avoid monotony, a 12 week 'strength' program, based on a 14 day cycle, will provide the right build-up to a period of racing. Within the 14 day cycle, you would include one session of long hills, two of medium hills, plus a session of hilly fartlek. The harder and longer the hill session, the easier the training must be the next day, until the athlete's body has learnt to cope. As the competition approaches, you should drop the hills to once a week, making the other days a more race-specific sessions.

The middle distance runner might drop the long hills, but keep the medium ones going until he/she starts the track training - even then, hills can be done once every two weeks to maintain strength. The runner who is trying to increase finishing speed might well want to keep the short hills going right through the early part of the track season. However, there must come a time when the main work becomes race-specific, and will be done on flat ground.

There is one situation where a hilly course can be used in the track or road racing season, and that is in the time trials or tempo runs in the last couple of weeks before a major event. You may want to do something to see how fit your athlete is and to test out their ability to push themselves. For a middle-distance runner, a grassy hill or a sand-dune course of, say, half-a-mile, is just the thing for a pre-race test. Running up a hill on a soft surface is much less damaging than doing, say, 1000m on a synthetic track, yet it gives all the pain and all the pleasure of a really hard work-out and that, after all, is what we are trying to achieve.

Downhill running

Many runners develop muscle soreness after strenuous workouts or races. For runners this would involve downhill running, since downhills put the muscles in the front of the leg under intense eccentric duress. A single downhill session (6 to 10 downhill runs over 300 metres) on a 300 to 400 metre hill with an inclination of 10 to 15 degrees should provide protection against muscle pain and loss of strength for at least six weeks.

With all hill sessions, it is important to warm up before and to cool down after the hill session - easy jog for 5 to 10 minutes followed by stretching exercises. Two sessions a week for six to eight weeks will improve your overall fitness and running speed.

Strength development

Session 1

— Need a hill with a slope of approx. 10% and a length of 200 metres to 400 metres
— Run up at approx 5km pace with rapid stride rate and good knee lift
— Recovery jog back down
— Start with 2 sets of 4 repetitions and gradually increase over time.

Session 2

— Need a hill with a slope of approx 5% and a length of 1km
— Run up at approx 10km pace with rapid stride rate and good knee lift
— Recovery jog back down
— Start with 3 or 4 repetitions and gradually increase over time.

Session 3 (treadmill)

— Treadmill at 3% incline
— Run up at approx 10km pace for 3 minutes
— 3 minute jog recovery
— Start with 3 or 4 repetitions and gradually increase over time.

Session 4 (treadmill)

— Set treadmill pace to your 10km pace and with no break.

— Run for 5 minutes with a 4% incline.

— Run for 10 minutes with a 5% incline.

— Run for 10 minutes with a 6% incline.

— Run for 10 minutes with a 7% incline.

Speed development

Over speed training can be achieved by running down a hill. The difficulty is finding a suitable hill with a safe surface.

— Need a hill with a slope of approx 15° decline and a length of 100m.

— Running down use 40 metres to 60 metres to build up to full speed and then maintain the speed for a further 30 metres.

— Recovery walk back up.

— Start with 2 sets of 4 repetitions and gradually increase over time.

4

Planning of Speed and Agility Training

Learning any new agility techniques can be like sensory overload for most athletes at the grade, middle and high school levels. Yet, like clockwork, they all attempt to perform the drill at top speed long before they are capable of doing it in a way that is not painful on the eyes. And that is putting it nicely, as I am sure you know. So, though it may seem overly simplified, as it pertains to agility training, the speed secret is: 'Slow down, master the technique, then build in the speed.'

Skill Development

You have to crawl before you can walk. But most athletes try to sprint before they can even crawl. Coordination is a significant impeding factor for many inexperienced athletes. Therefore it is critical that when learning or practicing an agility drill, they must often walk through the drill first, before trying to do it for time. This is true whether we are talking about cone drills, agility ladder work or any other change of direction, starting/stopping activities.

When first teaching any new agility drill, we will penalise athletes for making mistakes that are a result of trying to get ahead of themselves. Young athletes will always make mistakes - these are to be expected. But when they try to move their body faster than their brains can process, we have to slow them down so that they program the correct movement patterns into their system. In the long run, this will go a long way to improving their overall sports performance. Before we get into a practice session, we have to remember that the 40 yard dash (or 30 meter sprint) is not the only way to assess an athlete's speed. There is a difference between quick and fast. Someone that is considered fast may not necessarily be quick and vice-versa.

The best athletes have a combination of both quick and fast characteristics and they must train both. Lateral speed and agility work is a critical element to any athlete's training because it lays the foundation for the movement skills required for success in any sport. As I mentioned, lack of coordination is a big problem for many athletes. How many times have you seen a good athlete stumble when making a simple cut, performing a new skill, or better yet, try to dance? It happens far too often and it is all due to lack of coordination.

The inability to easily coordinate movement affects their footwork and their ability to quickly make the moves that top athletes seem to do naturally. Therefore, no matter what sport you coach, specific agility training will help develop the balance, coordination and timing that will allow athletes to get to the ball or away from the defender when the game is on the line. The following are examples of an agility drill and a reaction drill.

Agility drill - funnel drill

For this drill you will require 6 cones. The first 2 cones are next to each other 2 yards apart. Place cones 3 and 4, 3 yards away from the first 2 and separate them 4 yards apart. Cones 5 and 6 are going to be 3 yards away from cones 3 and 4, and they will be separated 6 yards apart. The cones should form a shape of a funnel.

Begin this drill in an athletic position in front of cone 1. On a command of a coach or training partner, laterally shuffle to cone 2. Touch the top of cone 2 then sprint diagonally to cone 3, touch, and then shuffle to cone 4. Touch cone 4 then sprint diagonally to cone 5, touch and laterally shuffle to cone 6. Touch cone 6 then sprint forward 5 yards to the finish line.

Be sure to maintain a good athletic stance for the duration of this drill. Keep the hips low and the toes pointed straight ahead. You will continuously see your athletes pointing the toe in the direction they are travelling. While this helps them move in that direction, they will be beaten every time if their opponent quickly changes direction on them.

Progressions

There are many different variations to this drill. You can add different cuts, moves and changes of direction to the funnel pattern. You can add different commands (audible or visual) to start the drill or to have the athlete perform different movements. To make this drill even more challenging, you can add an opponent or a ball, while making sure you are not compromising the technique of the drill. You know the strengths and weaknesses of your athletes, so add variety by changing the format of the drill. Your imagination truly is the only limitation to the variations of these types of drills. Since agility is also reacting to a stimulus, we must also train reaction.

Reaction drill - Tennis ball drop

A coach or training partner holds a tennis ball shoulder height. When the ball is released, the athlete must catch the ball before it bounces a second time. The coach/

training partner can change the distance they are standing or change the height of where they drop the tennis ball. Have your athletes attack the ball moving either laterally or in a linear direction.

Developing your Speed

'Long slow distance makes long slow runners.' What does that mean? From experience, the level of intensity (and therefore productivity) of these fun runs can be pretty low. There are more beneficial, less time consuming ways to improve aerobic conditioning than spending that time out running slow for a long time. Remember, train slowly to run slow. We are not saying that athletes in sports such as soccer, field hockey, lacrosse, etc., should not do any work on the roads. There are other ways to improve conditioning that can fulfil other training requirements at the same time.

Circuits

In the end, it does not matter how fast your athletes are if they are not in good enough shape to finish strong at the end of the game. Traditionally, coaches use running workouts to improve aerobic conditioning. However, those types of workouts only cover one of the many areas that are required to get athletes in great shape. That is why we use general strength circuits as a means of getting athletes in the overall condition that wins championships.

These circuits are usually bodyweight exercises that do not involve any external loading (weights). This type of workout not only provides the aerobic benefits that many running workouts give, but also helps the body both prepare for and recover from intense speed days and improve the physical strength. Additionally, the core strength that most young athletes lack can be properly addressed, as can improvements in balance and coordination, which is a major part of getting faster. There is only so much time in a day and any opportunity to accomplish multiple tasks in less time only means that athletes can spend extra time working on the particular skills of their individual sport.

We can use these workouts to develop core strength as well. For athletic purposes, the core consists of the abdominals, hips, gluteus, lower back, as well as the shoulders. The power required for maximal running, jumping and throwing is transferred through the core. If athletes neglect to train this area with consistency, strengths gains made from other areas of training are reduced significantly. It is not enough to do some crunches for the first two weeks of the season and then stop.

The entire core region must be trained in order to get the most out of any athlete's abilities. When training the core, especially the abdominals, be sure to focus on stabilisation exercises. When running, athletes must stabilise the torso to create maximal force and maintain technique.

General strength circuit

We are going to use a jump rope (skipping rope) in this circuit. The reason the jump rope was added, besides adding variety, is to help increase foot speed, work on balance/coordination, and increase aerobic capacity (work capacity). You combine all of those great benefits along with the benefits of doing general strength work listed above and you have created a completely efficient workout that will only take about 25 minutes! Jump Rope Circuit: (performed on grass)

— Jump Rope - 1 minute (30seconds - 2 feet, 30 seconds - Hip turns)

— Jog 50 yards
— Squats - 1x20
— Jog 50 yards
— Jump Rope - 1 minute (30 seconds Crossover, 30 seconds Double Skip)
— Jog 50 yards
— Burpees - 1x10
— Jog 50 yards
— Jump Rope - 1 minute (30 seconds Skip, 30 seconds High knee)
— Jog 50 yards
— Lunges - 10 each leg
— Jog 50 yards
— 3 minute break then repeat the circuit

When you repeat this exercise you can change the exercises (e.g. add lateral lunges, split squats, etc.) and also change the order of the jump rope exercise. Additionally, try switching core exercises for the jump rope exercises. For a more demanding workout, increase the pace of the jog between exercises.

Developing your Speed - Step over, Drive Down

Doing it well takes practice. You can get better at it, or make others better at it, simply by changing the way you use your muscles. The primary 'running muscles' are the gluteus and hamstrings. So it is critical that athletes learn to employ those muscle groups when performing speed work.

When doing any type of speed work, it is critical that your athletes learn to step over the opposite knee and drive the foot down into the ground so that it lands underneath the hips with each stride.

You understand the simple fact that speed is the single most important component of success in almost every sport. It seems like some people are born with it and some are not. Speed is a skill that can be taught. By training the body to move in certain ways, every athlete can make significant increases in their overall speed, which means the speed and success of the team as a whole can quickly take them to the next level.

When developing your athletes' acceleration skills, it is important to work on two key elements: mechanics and real speed work. In terms of mechanics, your athletes must perform the speed drills that reinforce the 'step over, drive down' principle. The purpose behind having them perform these drills and exercises is to reprogram their neuromuscular system to fire the muscles in the patterns that produce greater force and therefore greater speed.

Correct technique

Most athletes have never been taught to run the right way so they are very inefficient. One common technical problem is when athletes swinging their arms across their body instead of firing the elbow down and back. Another major problem affecting the vast majority of inexperienced athletes is called 'reaching'. This occurs during the recovery phase of running when an athlete allows the foot to travel out past the opposite knee. The result is that the athlete's foot reaches and lands out past their centre of mass causing a breaking action.

Watch your athletes when they practice or go watch some film of them competing. As they run, check or pause the video as soon as their foot touches the ground. If it is out past their hips instead of directly underneath the hips they are 'reaching' and running considerably slower than they are capable. Additionally, they are placing great stress on their hamstring because the muscle is not working in the way it is meant to. So if you are seeing hamstring pulls, lower back problems, calf and/or Achilles strains in your athletes, especially as the season wears on, there is a good chance that part of the problem stems from poor running mechanics. One way to start to fix this problem is by giving your athletes cues to think about during practice, they will begin to reprogram their movement patterns and immediately get faster.

For example, to fix the reaching problem cue them to 'step over the opposite knee and drive down.' Other ways to say this are 'run through tall grass' and 'run through knee high water'. Greater speeds are produced by applying more force to the ground. By learning to drive the foot straight down, landing underneath the hips, athletes will make the most of their existing strength levels and reduce injury.

Speed development

The next element to consider when developing the speed hidden within your athletes is making sure you are doing real speed workouts with them. Speed work is defined as 2 to 8 seconds if high intensity work followed by full recovery. That means they must rest at least 2 to 3 minutes between each repetition!

Running at full speed is extremely taxing on the Central Nervous System. If the body does not recover fully, athletes will quickly break down and lose the ability to move in the optimal patterns. If they try to sprint in a state of fatigue, they will not improve acceleration or top speed, they will only get better at running at 85-90%. These workouts have a time and a place, but they will not make your athletes faster.

Think about how you are training your athletes. Do your workouts accomplish the objective you are aiming for? Are they getting enough rest between intervals? Are their running mechanics sound? Are you experiencing a high volume of injuries? These are all issues to seriously consider when evaluating your current program.

Because most sports involve short bursts of speed with low intensity activity, followed by short bursts of speed we will focus on acceleration development. Learning how to overcome our own body weight and accelerate to full speed as quickly and efficiently as possible separates starters from bench warmers, champions from 'also rans'. Here is a sample speed session, focusing on acceleration development. Cue athletes to get up as quickly as possible.

— 4 x 30 yards from a push up - down position (rest 2 minutes between each rep)
— 5 minute rest between sets
— 6 x 30 yards in a kneeling position - 3 left/3 right (rest 2 minutes between each rep)

We like to have athletes start in various positions starting from the ground because they require the athlete to generate more force than a regular standing start.

Developing your Speed - Learn to Land Softly and Quietly

This month's speed secret is both a cue for your athletes and a foundational concept for applying plyometric training to your program: "Learn to land softly and quietly. Absorb each landing with the muscles in your legs so you do not place extreme stress on joints, bones, ligaments and tendons." If athletes are making loud noises with their feet or landing stiffly, then they are not performing the exercise correctly. Always err on the side of caution when using plyometrics.

Of course, when done correctly, plyometrics are an excellent supplement to your speed, strength and power training program. They can greatly improve your power levels and help increase body control since they deal with moving your own bodyweight. I am sure you have done, or had your athletes do; bounding exercises, box jumps or medicine ball throws before. The question is: how do you know whether athletes are actually benefiting from these activities as opposed to putting themselves at risk for injury?

Athletes always want to do the most advanced, most technical movements that they see the professional athletes doing in their training. However, because these exercises require so much power and coordination, there needs to be a careful progression in the structure plyometric training. It may not be glorious and exciting, but in the short and long term, learning to evolve from basic to complex movements will always reap the greatest rewards. If we jump right into single leg bounds or depth jumps, without the proper progression, then we are putting our athletes at risk for avoidable injury.

Most young athletes lack one of, all of, or a combination of the following: balance, coordination, flexibility, power, muscular strength and core strength. Think about where you, your team or your athletes have weaknesses. To benefit from plyometrics, athletes must be strong in all of the aforementioned areas. If they try to perform high intensity plyometrics before they are ready, they will get injured.

We know of athletes, especially male athletes, trying to imitate professional athletes by insisting that they can do single leg hurdle hops over 39 hurdles and other crazy manoeuvres only to land awkwardly and ruin their brief careers with a knee injury or the like.

As a coach you have to look at the three ages of your athlete to determine what level of plyometric training to use with your team.

When determining the level of plyometric training to apply to your athletes, you must look at their "three ages" to make an informed decision. Those ages are their training age (how many years have they been actively training), their biological age (what is their physical maturation in years) and their chronological age (years they have been alive).

Young kids run and jump and do the equivalent of plyometrics from a young age. I would not have a 12 year old boy doing alternate leg bounds with a 10yard run up, but I would have them do double leg stabilisation work or maybe even double leg bounds depending on the aforementioned factors.

Another factor to look at with plyometrics is the athlete's strength to body weight ratio. A 16 year old girl who weighs 125lbs but can squat 175lbs, has greater relative strength than a 16 year old boy who weighs 180lbs, but squats 200lbs. Physically the boys are stronger, but their ability to control that weight at full speed might not be as great as his 'weaker' female counterpart. Again, plyometrics can greatly increase strength, power, body control and awareness, etc. But it has to be carefully introduced to an athlete's program.

Stabilisation

Remember, you must learn how to stabilise and absorb forces appropriately. The key is to land softly and absorb the forces created with the muscles (not the joints!). If you are landing quietly then you are probably on the right path.

Drills

Box Jumps - Start with a 12 inch box. Once the soft landing is perfected, increase box height as appropriate. After jumping up and achieving triple extension (full extension of the ankles, knees and hips), land on the box (quietly) and absorb the impact by landing in a quarter to half-squat position (not stiff-legged). Perform 3 sets of 5 repetitions.

Single Leg Lateral Hops - Standing on 1 leg, jump laterally over a cone, gaining moderate height. Land on the opposite leg and absorb the impact with the muscles. Stabilise for 2 full seconds and then alternate. Perform 3 sets of 10 repetitions (5 on each leg).

As a more advanced variation, perform this exercise by landing on the same leg you jump with. You may think these exercises are extremely basic, but I invite you to try them out with your athletes or by yourself and see how difficult it is to land softly and keep your balance!

Use these drills anywhere from 2-4 weeks, depending on your ability to land appropriately before progressing to the more advanced plyometrics. Please do not try and progress too quickly; remember, the more efficient you are at controlling and applying force, the faster and more powerful you will be!

Also, when first starting out, keep the number of contacts (times the feet hit the ground) to between 40 and 60 for the entire workout. Plyometrics are taxing on the nervous system and require full recovery, so treat rest like you would for speed work.

Developing your Speed — Flexibility

Most athletes (especially male athletes) will give their best effort for 95% of practice. But when it comes to stretching out after a workout or competition, they are nowhere to be found. In the first article, I went over why static stretching before your workout makes you slower and why dynamic activities provide more benefits. Remember? Good! Let us talk about stretching after training or competition. The best time to stretch is after intense activity when the body is warm and the muscles have a good blood flow. It is during this time that you can expect to make your biggest gains in range of motion and muscle flexibility.

Practice does not end until after flexibility work is completed

Too often, post practice flexibility work consists of athletes sitting together in a group with outstretched legs, not stretching but having a conversation! These athletes have just worked hard to become better and instead of finishing the session the right way, they are only adding to poor flexibility by allowing themselves to get tight. Remember, poor flexibility leads to reduced range of motion which means you reduce your stride length. Additionally, chronically tight muscles lead to a greater frequency of muscle spasms, strains and pulls, most of which can be avoided by taking 5 to 10 minutes to stretch. In this article we will focus on one of the four proven techniques that many athletes use to increase their flexibility - hurdle drills.

Hurdle mobility drills

Hurdle drills will help you increase the range of motion in your hips. Many athletes are extremely limited in their range of motion in this area which means they are going to be running slower than they are capable of. Line up 5 hurdles and set them to the lowest height. The spacing between each hurdle will depend on the height and/or flexibility of the athlete. Start with 3 feet between each hurdle and adjust from there. Repeat each exercise 4 times.

Walkovers

Stand up tall and step over each hurdle, keeping your knee up when stepping over and make sure you are not swinging the foot around the hurdle. Focus on driving the knee up so that the shin stays perpendicular to the ground at all times. As a variation to Walkovers have them walk backwards over the hurdles.

Laterals

Starting with the hips perpendicular to the hurdle, drive your knee up to step over the middle of the hurdle. Lead with the right leg twice and the left leg twice.

Over and under

Step over the first hurdle like you did in the walkovers. As you pull the trail leg over, pivot with your first foot so that the hips are perpendicular to the hurdle and step under hurdle number 2 with your second foot. Drop your hips so you can get low enough to be able to step and make it through underneath the second hurdle. Repeat until you have completed the 5 hurdles. This is a phenomenal exercise for opening up your hips and a great way to end your practices!

How to Increase Your Speed — Acceleration

Speed is a product of stride length and stride frequency. However, you will not reach top speed by focusing on increasingly larger steps to increase stride length or taking short, quick steps to increase stride frequency. Instead, top speeds are created by applying 'optimal' force to the ground. Both length and frequency are improved by strength so better strength application results in faster speeds. Really, acceleration training is a form of strength training.

Ground contact times are another important factor to consider during acceleration. During the earliest parts of acceleration, especially the first two steps, you are trying to overcome (inertia) the weight of your body by moving it forward as quickly as possible. This takes a great deal of strength and power. The stronger and more efficient you are, the more you can extend your acceleration phase.

High intensity sprint work involves recruiting specific groups of muscle fibres and improves the efficiency of neuromuscular firing patterns. Sprinting is taxing to the central nervous system (CNS) and once the CNS becomes fatigued, workouts quickly lose their effectiveness. Any type of speed work must be done with full recovery - approximately one minute of rest for every 10 metres that you run. Sprinting is a highly technical activity.

Without full recovery, both your muscles and your CNS will begin to fatigue quickly, reducing the short and long-term effectiveness of your training. For this reason, acceleration should not be trained with fatigue present. To optimise your success, full recovery must be adhered to both in your individual workouts as well as your weekly plan. It takes roughly 36-48 hours to recover from a speed workout.

Acceleration cues

— Drive the lead arm (same as front leg) up as you begin to sprint
— Drive out so the body is at a 45° angle to the ground
— Keep the heel recovery low during the first 6-8 strides
— Drive the elbows down and back. Keep the hands loose, but not open
— Arms should remain at approximately 90 degrees at the elbow
— Step over the opposite knee and drive the foot down into the ground to create maximal force
— Do not force yourself to 'stay low'. This will limit the amount of force you can apply to the ground and leads to poor acceleration

— Let your upper body unfold naturally. 'Staying low' will occur naturally if you are already strong enough

During acceleration, the foot should strike directly below or slightly behind the hips. You must be able to drive out so your body is at a 45° angle to the ground, step over the opposite knee, and drive the foot down into the ground to create maximal force.

Acceleration work should be used at the beginning of your training season. You cannot be efficient running longer distances without getting the proper strength levels and neuromuscular efficiency off the shorter intervals. You want to be driving out as far as possible so the stronger you are the further the acceleration phase will be which in turn will improve your top speed.

Improve your Sprinting Speed

Keeping it simple while being effective is the challenge with developing most fitness components and improving sprinting speed is no exception to this. Breaking things down into a series of manageable chunks usually makes things easier. For sprinting we might consider a logical order for progression to be:

Correct running (striding)

The initial priority is to ensure correct sprinting while remaining almost upright otherwise all training sessions will only serve to further ingrain any lack of technique. Developing a technique that is optimal for the athlete may take a long time but is crucial for maintenance of top speed. In some cases we may have to 'fix' poor points, even undo some long-established habits - this can require 'neural remodelling' as well as the more obvious physical development and we must be persistent and patient. Energy systems dictate that all athletes start to slow down after 5-8 seconds. Striding is about developing a sprinting action that serves to minimise energy losses and hence minimises the inevitable speed losses. Key elements:

— *Leg 'cycling'* - Biomechanics of 'foot lifting and cycling' rather than 'knee lifting'
— *Lightness of contact* - maximise energy return / minimise energy loss / maximise biomechanics
— Focus on ball of foot contact
— *Posture* - relating to core strength / warning signs may include hips sunken - leading to early foot strike and loss of energy
— *Balance*- relating to core strength / poor proprioception / lack of bilateral development - warning signs may include torso rotation, foot plant 'cross-over' and a non-linear path
— *Relaxation* - minimise energy usage / maintain biomechanics. Sometimes seen most obviously in the shoulders and neck area leading to imbalance in the upper body and arm cross-over in front
— *Appropriate use of drills* - range of movement, contact, posture

Poor striding leads to premature loss of maximum speed attained during the acceleration phase.

Accelerating

The objective of acceleration is to attain maximum speed in as short a time as possible. Key elements:

— Set position - biomechanics
— Pushing the centre of gravity - assuming a near linear posture from head to toe with a forward lean
— Leg speed and extension of stride
— Appropriate power / explosivity energy system training

— Appropriate drills - leg speed, range of movement, power development

Transitioning to stride

The key here is to move from a powerful forward leaning position held during acceleration through to the relaxed upright position of striding without sacrificing speed. The key to transition is 'smooth' over as fewer strides as appropriate.

Starting

This is specific to track sprinters and requires developing the best position biomechanically (for the skill) and anthropometrically (for their body) to allow the maximal and fastest drive from the blocks. Reaction and response are the key factors to move swiftly into the acceleration position.

Lifting

The final piece in the sprinters armoury is to slightly modify technique in the final drive to the line - many female sprinters accomplish this with a slight quickening of tempo through shortening of action. Male sprinters often find a deliberately longer drive of the arms can work to extend the stride. Neither serve to reaccelerate only minimise speed loss. Both appear to have merits depending, not necessarily, on the gender of the athlete.

How to Improve the Function of the Hamstring Muscles for Speed

We specifically take a look at the group of three hamstring muscles that run down the back of the leg. The muscles include the semimembranosus, the semitendinosus, and the biceps femoris. These muscles bend (flex) the leg at the knee and also straighten (extend) the leg at the hip joint. They are especially important for effective sprinting in terms of power and stride length. The way these muscles function and the forces that result from speed work or sprinting may lead to injury to this muscle group if insufficient flexibility has been developed (they do control stride length), poor strength is present (particularly relative to the opposing - antagonistic - quadriceps muscle group to the front of the leg) or else basic biomechanics are at fault.

Injuries reduced

The reality is that provided sufficient and appropriate strengthening work has been carried out in parallel with flexibility development then the biomechanics of sprinting are better supported. The potential for injury is also significantly reduced. Despite an ever-increasing body of sometimes conflicting information on when and what to stretch there still remain vague or even inaccurate guidelines on 'how to' stretch and indeed 'why'.

Planning

Identifying poor flexibility in the hamstrings is not always as easy as may be imagined since other factors may be involved including poor technique, other restrictions or a history of injury. However, once a coach or trainer knows the athlete they are working with then consistency in performance can usually be established and any limiting factors clearly identified such as short stride length. Consultation with a qualified Physiotherapist at this stage is always a good step to confirm beliefs and to help bring out any history of injury in this area. Stretching should follow the principle of regular controlled progressive static stretching of fully warmed-up muscle in sessions largely run separately to other training sessions along with the integration of suitable dynamic stretching activities as part of normal session warm-up.

Assessment

Use of the classical 'sit and reach test' can help to establish current hamstring flexibility and be used to set a target for improvement within an agreed time.

Exercises - static stretching

There are many examples in the literature of hamstring stretches. However, many of these cases fail to take account of modern best practice (how long, how often, when etc), contra-indications (opposite knee under pressure in 'hurdles' position or arching of the spine, for example) and specificity (what is actually being stretched). The best single, most effective, safe and specific hamstring group stretch from personal experience and the advice of Physiotherapists is the seated, bent leg stretch as shown in figure 1.

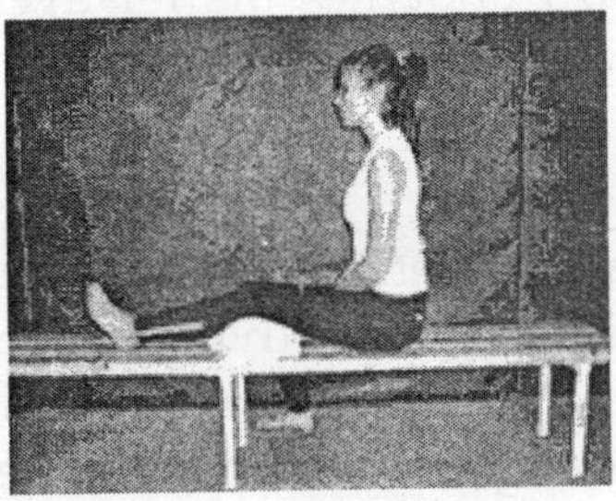

Relaxed

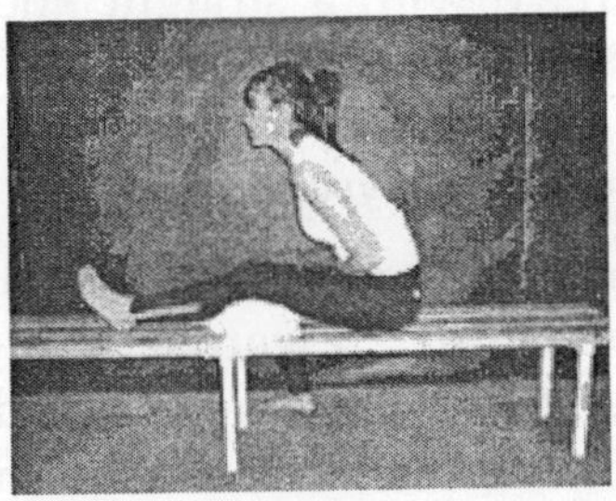

Extended

Figure 1 - The seated bent knee hamstring stretch

How to start

Sit comfortably on a bench or similar support that allows the foot of the free leg to rest comfortably on the ground. Position a suitable support - e.g. cushion under the knee of the leg to be worked to ensure a partially flexed knee is maintained. Sit 'tall' with hips neutral and move the whole upper body forward toward the leg keeping alignment throughout - there is simply no need to stretch out with the arms or to grasp the shin for example - often this just leads to poor posture and an ineffective stretch! Hold the stretch for 10 seconds and repeat 3 times. Work both legs in turn.

Progression

Extend the hold time to 20-30 seconds. Increase the number of repetitions in a session up to 10. Increase the frequency of stretching to several times per week. Use the 'sit and reach test' to determine improvement. Re-assess every 6 weeks or so.

This stretch has a number of advantages including - a comfortable position, there is no unnecessary strain elsewhere in the body, specificity - it stretches the hamstring muscle. Maybe the prevalence of guidelines to stretch with a straight knee also underlies the relatively high injury rate?

Exercises - dynamic stretching

Progression to a specific dynamic stretching activity can reap great rewards. Using the standing dynamic 'leg cycling' drill is great for developing coordination, rapid contraction and relaxation through an extended range (flexibility) and for developing specific hamstring strength / power (figure 2). Recent research has highlighted the fact that in sprinting the biceps femoris muscle is the last of the group of three hamstring muscles to 'fire' during the sprint cycle and is often left exposed at the end of the support phase leading to injury if there are limitations in flexibility, strength and coordination present.

Start *Drive Down* *Recovery*

Figure 2 - Phases of the leg cycling drill

How to start

A good start is to work on 3 sets of 10 cycles at around 1 cycle every 2 seconds, slowly lifting the knee so that the upper leg is presented parallel to the ground and then driving the leg back and downwards in a rapid controlled movement with the foot kept fully flexed at the ankle (dorsiflexed). The ball of the foot should be allowed to just contact the ground. To best match the specifics of movement in sprinting the leg should be actively 'recovered' as soon as the foot touches the ground and is directly below the body i.e. it should not be allowed to swing out of control behind the body - this takes practice! Work both legs evenly unless seeking to address an imbalance!

Progression

This activity can be made progressive in terms of the cycling rate (up 3 per second), the duration (up to 15 seconds), the range of movement (particularly knee lift and height of foot recovery or knee flexion) and the focus within the cycle (developing to a smooth complete cycling action).

Speed Development - more than just Running Fast

Speed is the capacity to perform successive movements at a fast rate. As well as thinking about speed as "running speed" it is really the development of the ability to move the limbs quickly which is needed in a variety of sports and events e.g. javelin, discus, tennis, squash etc. Therefore, there is more to think about than just running fast.

Energy system for speed

Energy for absolute speed is supplied by the anaerobic alactic pathway. The anaerobic (without oxygen) alactic (without lactate) energy system is best challenged as an athlete approaches top speed between 30 and 60 metres while running at 95% to 100% of maximum.

Developing Speed

They say that sprinters are "born and not made" due to the necessity of having a preponderance of fast twitch muscle fibres. The development of pure speed involves stimulating the central nervous system to send messages through to the muscles to tell them to contract. The speed of this contraction has a significant bearing on the power of the movement.

When applied in the field of sport however this "element of speed" is not enough on its own. Genetically our muscles comprise of a certain level of fast/slow twitch fibres, which does not significantly change.

In racquet sports like tennis and field events like the javelin, limb speed is essential but strength, suppleness, stamina and skill all play a part in the application of speed to the field of performance. Speed is therefore an element of the conditioning of the body to meet the specific needs of the sport, but how do we develop it? As a track coach, my sprinters use a variety of exercises and drills to stimulate the responses needed within the body to run fast.

Reaction speed

Reaction runs are useful to develop and improve the ability to react quickly and move from any position to a sprint in the least possible time. Everyone will be able to think of starting positions that correlate to a position that their performers would get into. Progression of this training can be made with weighted jackets or other forms of resistance (weighted sledge, tyre).

Over speed training

Downhill sprinting is an ideal way to developing sprinting speed. A hill with a maximum of a 15° decline is most suitable. Use 40 metres to 60 metres to build up to full speed and then maintain the speed for a further 30 metres. A session could comprise of 2 to 3 sets of 3 to 6 repetitions. The difficulty with this method is to find a suitable hill with a safe surface. Over-speed work could be carried out on the track when there are prevailing strong winds - run with the wind behind you.

Speed workouts for a selection of running events

Event	*Speed Session*
100 metres	10 × 30 metres at race pace from blocks with full recovery3 to 4 × 80 metres at race pace with full recovery
800 metres	5 × 200 metres at goal race pace with 10 seconds recovery4 × 400 metres at 2 to 3 seconds faster than current race pace with 2 minutes recovery
1500 metres	4 × 400 metres at goal race pace with 15 to 10 sec recovery4 to 5 × 800 metres at 5 to 6 seconds per 800 metres faster than goal race pace with 6 minutes recovery

5,000 metres	4 to 5 × 800 metres at 4 seconds per 800 metres faster than goal race pace with 60 seconds recovery3 × 1 mile at 6 seconds per mile faster than goal race pace with 2 minutes recovery
10,000 metres	3 × 2000 metres at 3 seconds per 200 metres faster than goal race pace with 2 minutes recoveryFive 5 min intervals at current 5km race pace with 3 minutes recovery
Marathon	Six 1 mile repeats at 15 seconds per mile faster that goal race pace with 1 minute recovery3 × 3000 metres at 10km race pace with 6 minutes recovery

When should speed work be conducted? It is important to remember that the improvement of running speed is a complex process, which is controlled by the brain and nervous system. In order for a runner to move more quickly, the leg muscles of course have to contract more quickly, but the brain and nervous systems have to learn to control these faster movements efficiently.

If you maintain some form of speed training throughout the year, your muscles and nervous system do not lose the feel of moving fast and the brain will not have to re-learn the proper control patterns at a later date. In the training week, speed work should be carried out after a period of rest or light training. In a training session, speed work should be conducted after the warm up and any other training should be of a low intensity.

Sprinting technique

Most sports will involve the need to generate speed at some point. On the track, sprinters hone their sprint technical skills in concert with speed, as good technique will greatly enhance the speed that is generated. The technique used in running fast may need to be adapted e.g. in rugby a winger may wish not to run quite as relaxed as he might on a track in order to brace himself for a tackle.

5

Designing an Effective Speed Training Programme

What are the demands of your sport and, thus, the speed, strength and conditioning requirements? Without having a clear understanding of this foundational question, you cannot possibly design an effective program for anyone. Let us break this question down a little bit further so that there is no confusion.

Planning and Organising your Sport's Practice and Training Activities

The following questions will help you understand the mindset you must bring to planning and organising your sport's practice and training activities.

1. How long does a game/competition take?

The training plan for a 55-meter sprinter and a soccer player cannot be the same. One athlete may be competing for up to 90 minutes, the other for less than 7 seconds.

2. What is the rest period between plays/events?

Would the rest intervals for a track sprinter, who may have an hour or more off between events, be the same as a football player who only has 30-40 seconds between plays?

3. What is the ratio between sprinting, jogging and walking during a competition?

Soccer and field hockey players need to be able to sprint at short bursts then go into a jog, repeatedly, for an extended period. Would interval training be more useful for these athletes or continuous slow distance training? Acceleration is critical to the success of these athletes but how often do they specifically build this necessary skill into their programs?

4. What type of 'speed' do you need to succeed at your sport?

There is a difference between just doing some speed work and actual speed development. The former is what is occasionally done in some programs. The latter is specifically designed to foster adaptations that improve the skill of sprinting over time.

Do the demands of your sport focus on acceleration like soccer, football, lacrosse and basketball or does the ability to maintain near top speeds determine success, like for a 200-meter sprinter? Acceleration development and maximum velocity training must be addressed differently. What about speed versus speed endurance? Faster top speeds can only be developed when there is no presence of fatigue. While both skills need to be trained, some sports require athletes to be able to accelerate or change directions while under a state of fatigue.

After all, there is a world of difference between these two seemingly similar workouts: 1. 10x30m @ 100% intensity with 3 minutes rest 2. 10x30m @ 100% intensity with 30 seconds rest One will improve an athlete's ability to get from point A to Point B in the shortest time possible. The other will improve an athlete's ability to get from Point A to Point B in the shortest average time possible, with decreasing difference between the fastest and slowest times.

5. What sport specific and speed specific skills must be factored into your training plan?

How many times in a game do your basketball players or volleyball players have to jump? How many times in a row will they have to jump in most situations? Many athletes will do sustained vertical jumps for periods of 30+ seconds as the sole means of improving specific 'jumping' or 'vertical leaping' ability. How many times do these athletes have to jump in a row? Would they not make better improvements to their maximum vertical leap height by practicing a few jumps at full intensity, then resting? How does jumping endurance help an athlete out rebound their opponent or spike the ball in a single effort situation? If my team does Workout A and yours does Workout B, whose athletes are going to succeed in getting more rebounds, blocks or kills over time?

— 4 sets of five jump squats with 3-4 minutes rest

— 3 sets of 30 seconds sustained jump squats with one-minute rest

From here, we can keep adding details to the training demands such as looking at the energy system and metabolic demands. However, when you use common sense, it really is not that complicated. Now that you are beginning to understand the specific demands of your sport, we have to look at two things in order to identify why this process is so important to athletic success:

— Why we train in the first place

— What organised training actually does for the body

While conclusions made during a discussion of these two issues may seem painfully obvious once explained, one only has to look at the lack of organisation and forethought behind most strength and conditioning programs to understand that such issues are hardly being taken into consideration when most plans are being created. That is why, when in doubt, we go back to the basics.

So, why do we train? At its most basic level, we train to overcome fatigue. During the course of any competition, athletes are going to get tired. By using certain specific training modalities, athletes can learn to overcome that fatigue, or at least delay it long enough to succeed. Many people think (or are taught) that you will experience the greatest success in this race by running the entire distance as hard and as fast as humanly possible. However, that is just not possible. A sprinter must 'rest' or 'float' during the race to conserve energy. This subtle skill takes patience and experience, but is nonetheless true. By the midpoint of the race, most athletes are in fact, slowing down. When you step back and look at the entire picture, the 100-meter dash, like most competitions, is won by the athlete who decelerates the slowest.

By using certain specific training modalities, the 100-meter runner can learn to overcome some of the fatigue that sets in by training him/herself to decelerate slower than the competition. Now, it is the job of the 100-meter athlete to factor in this fact to the their training by understanding the demands of the event.

Of course, slowing down the slowing down is just one of many elements of the 100-meter dash but without specifically addressing this fact, athletes cannot reach their potential. Therefore, the coach/athlete must consider what methods he/she can use to address this issue, one of many limiting factors that must be understood and dealt with in order to develop the fastest possible athletes.

Another Reason we Train is to Perfect Technique

Repetition of a properly executed skill will train the athlete to perform automatically, a critical skill when considering the amount of information athletes must process during the course of any competitive situation. This too must be addressed in a specific fashion worked into the framework of the overall training plan. The main reason we train, above all else, is to improve performance. Often, to improve so that we are competing at our best at the end of the season for the state championship, playoff tournament, Super Bowl, etc.

At other times, especially in team-based sports like football and basketball, athletes must be in top shape at the start of the regular season. The season is all about maintaining all the improvements that were made in the preseason. This difference, however, in no way changes the approach that should be taken to creating the speed development program. Regardless of the sport, clearly many factors go into a season. Your job is to ensure that your training program allows you to be at your best when the time comes. The best way to maximise the likelihood of this occurring is to organise your training by carefully following the framework that is being laid out in this series.

The next issue of importance deals with what organised training techniques actually do to the body, especially in comparison to the generally unorganised training that most coaches employ. This will go far in helping to understand just how significant the level of improvement can be when incorporating organised skill development into each microcycle, mesocycle and macrocycle. In the next article, we will explore this issue and look more specifically at the most important principles and components to designing an effective training program. For a speed-training program, it is important to determine where the focus is for your sport during the preseason and competitive season. We can break sports down into two categories:

1. Team sports e.g. football, rugby, hockey
2. Individual sports e.g. squash, Track and Field

Team sports like football, basketball and rugby are going to have to focus the majority of speed and conditioning development in the preseason. Once the competitive season starts the focus is likely going to be more on maintenance of the improvements made during the off season and preseason as opposed to specifically trying to make significant speed gains during the competitive season.

The problem see with team sports is that there is no organised periodisation or progression of conditioning in the preseason or competitive season. This is why there is often a rash of burnout, mid season performance regression (due to overtraining) and late season injuries. The techniques you will learn here should prevent that from happening ever again.

On the other side, you have 'individual' sports, where we will consider track and field. Here we often train through early season competitions with the goal being to have athletes run their fastest at the end of the season, instead of the beginning of the season like in team sports.The training principles for both categories are the same. Before you can begin creating a specific training plan, you have to be organised.

1. Establish a clear, specific goal for the training plan

This is the same whether designing a plan for an individual person or a team. Is the goal to improve your 40-metre time by 0.3 seconds by the start of the season? Do you want to win a State Title in the? Do you want to compete in the national school's championships in August?

If you identify a goal such as 'make myself quicker' then how will you know if you have accomplished it?

You have to set a time related measurable goal. This is one of the most overlooked and difficult components of the training plan. However, if you do not start with the end goal, end date, and work backwards, you cannot get a true understanding of how to progress your training.

2. Make a detailed analysis of the demands of your sport

Consider for your sport:

— Is there a significant anaerobic and/or aerobic demand to your sport?

— How about agility and change of direction skills

— Does your sport focus on acceleration or top end speed?

— Do you hold, swing or carry an implement in your sport?

3. Establish a list of qualities and abilities needed to succeed in the specific speed applications of your sport

This should be based upon your analysis of demands. For example:

— absorb impact and then accelerate

— accelerate while in a state of extreme fatigue

— develop consistent acceleration pattern out of blocks

— hit a moving ball while running at top speed

4. Create a list of specific training activities

This list should be designed to address and develop the identified list of qualities and abilities. For example:

— specific drills teaching how to take a hit and effectively accelerate

— fartlek runs and whistle workouts to simulate the types of starting and stopping while fatigued that they'll experience in a game

- drive phase development and block work session to teach a consistent, explosive sprint start
- drills developing techniques for striking, kicking or dribbling the ball while running at full speed

5. Create a list of general training activities

These should be designed to prepare the body to undertake specific training. For example:

- an athlete must learn how to separately absorb contact and learn to accelerate before the actions can effectively be combined
- athletes must develop their aerobic power, lactic capacity and acceleration ability before they can succeed at combining those three elements successfully
- athletes must develop a consistent acceleration pattern, understand the drive phase and perfect running mechanics before successfully developing a fast start
- athletes must learn how to kick, strike or dribble the ball, as well as learn acceleration and top speed mechanics before they can combine these skills

6. Organise the list of general and specific training activities into a logical training program

With any speed program, skills must go from general to specific, basic to complex. Athletes must establish general conditioning before doing complex lactic acid workouts. They must develop the ability to accelerate before doing speed endurance. In addition, these skills must be broken down further as well as addressing other fitness components that we will discuss shortly.

7. The training program must actually be administered and should undergo constant evaluation

Even the best plans must be modified. Weather, injuries, and a myriad of other situations and circumstances will arise that force you to change what you are doing. Sometimes you plan just plain does not work. That is why a detailed plan, as well as note taking and testing, will give you a good idea if your plan is progressing as expected.

Go through these seven steps and make specific notes on how they can be specifically applied to your sport or event. Bear in mind that even these seven topics are just a general overview of the pre-planning behind the training plan. Once you have established your lists, focus on the general areas that must be developed then you can start to get more specific.

Fitness Components

First, you must understand where the specificity comes from and why it is applied. In developing the speed of any athletes in any sport there are five fitness components that must be developed, regardless of the perceived differences between the sport/s being trained, age, gender and skill level of the athletes. These five fitness components are:

1. Speed
2. Strength
3. Coordination
4. Flexibility
5. Conditioning

And this is true regardless of sport, age, talent or experience. It is important that these 5 abilities be trained to some degree in every workout. However, depending on the time of year, sport and individual training goals, some will need to be trained more frequently than others. So let us review and cover these 5 fitness components before getting into the specific program design. The 5 bio-motor abilities are:

1. Flexibility
2. Coordination
3. Endurance
4. Strength
5. Speed

Flexibility

The need for flexibility varies by sport and event as well as from muscle group to muscle group. However, rarely have seen an athlete who appears to be 'too flexible.' However, lack of flexibility is an ever present issue. For our purposes there are two types of flexibility that we must address in our program:

1. Static flexibility
2. Dynamic flexibility

The need for static stretching before a workout or competition is a subject for debate and, like many training factors, is a matter of preference. However, static stretching as the sole means of improving mobility before a game or practice is a recipe for disaster. Excessive static stretching is known to decrease short term strength and power output so it cannot be the primary method of preparation for activities requiring strength and power output. Save static stretching for after practice as this is where the biggest gains in flexibility will be made. Dynamic mobility exercises must be the foundation of any practice or competitive situation. Dynamic stretching ensures muscles will be appropriately warmed up and the core body temperature is raised.

Co-ordination

The lack of co-ordination is one of the single greatest limiting factors to the success of young athletes, even the 'best' ones. Development of coordinative abilities is a requirement for success in all sports. These abilities include:

1. To spatially orient oneself
2. To kinaesthetically differentiate
3. To react
4. To keep rhythm
5. To maintain balance

In addition, co-coordinative ability develops before sexual maturity. Thus, it is believed that these skills must be developed during pre-pubescence since they are seen to regress during puberty. There are an infinite number of activities that develop the coordinative abilities including, but not limited to:

— change of direction drills
— agility ladder work
— dynamic exercises
— hurdle mobility
— plyometrics
— proprioceptive work
— speed drills
— medicine ball throws
— strength training
— sport specific activities (block work, batting practice running routes, running approaches, kicking a ball, etc)

All of these activities, when structured correctly within the overall macrocycle (yearly plan), will develop the co-ordination required to succeed on the track, court or field.

Endurance

Endurance is the capacity to maintain a certain degree of speed in the presence of fatigue. Specific endurance requirements vary by sport. Sending a football player or 100 meter runner out to run 3 miles is an unacceptable waste of time, but entirely appropriate for a soccer player or miler. We can break down endurance into two broad categories:

1. General Endurance
2. Specific Endurance

General endurance is ultimately the ability to maintain a level of performance for an extended period of time. It includes the neuromuscular, central nervous and cardio-respiratory endurance systems. General endurance is often equated with aerobic endurance because of its long term nature. Specific endurance refers to the unique endurance required to perform activities from playing football to running the marathon. Different sports require different specific endurance and knowledge of physiology allows you to design training specific to your sporting needs.

Strength

Strength is another requirement of optimal speed that is often either ignored or performed incorrectly. Common sense tells us that athletes can not expect to get faster if they do not get stronger. This is simply due to the fact that they will be unable to move their bodies forward due to limitations in their force output. There are, of course, different types of strength. Absolute strength is the ability to produce great force, regardless of the speed of movement. This quality is fundamental to all types of strength and governs the body's ability to control internally generated forces.

Power, the product of strength and speed, is the ability to produce force quickly. Overcoming one's bodyweight quickly is critical to acceleration, the fundamental element of speed development. General strength is the ability to control one's body and overcome internal resistance. Think of it as a combination of strength and coordination. This is a critical area of development for young (high school and below) athletes who either lack this type of strength or focus on developing other areas and neglecting this area, at a cost. Use general strength for postural stability, a substitute for weight training, endocrine system development, coordination and recovery.

Speed

A traditional definition of speed is: 'The ability to move the body and/or its parts quickly.' As with all training, I look at the demands of the activity in regards to its energy system requirements. We can break speed down into the following categories:

— Acceleration: 0 - 40 meters (0 - 5 seconds)
— Maximum Velocity: 40 - 80 meters (5 - 8 seconds)
— Speed Endurance: 80 - 150 meters
— Special Endurance I: 150 - 300 meters
— Special Endurance II: 300 - 600 meters

Outside of track and field, most athletes will not focus much time and energy beyond speed endurance. Take the time to consider how these 5 bio-motor abilities should be factored into your training. One of the main problems that many coaches and athletes have in training speed is that they are looking at the topic through a very narrow lens. Maximal speed development is far more than just running some 40s. With bio-motor development, every single microcycle should address all 5 bio-motor abilities to some extent.

But where you are in your training plan will determine the degree of emphasis that should be placed there. Everything you do in your training must be done for a reason. We live in a universe based on order. Everything that happens for a reason that, given enough time, can be specifically identified. That is why each element of an effective speed training program must be based, ultimately, on sound scientific and physiological principles. There are 6 fundamental training principles that I think should be addressed so far as continuing to build a foundation for understanding how you should approach designing a speed training program.

1. Adaptation

In essence, adaptation is the adjustment or enhancement of fitness that comes from your specific speed training protocols. Proper adaptation is the effect of relatively stable changes caused by the training sessions you implement. Examples are the reduced resting heart rate seen following an endurance training program and the increase in muscle fibre diameter after a period of strength training. The effectiveness of your adaptation stems from the effectiveness of your training. Keep in mind, however, that rate of adaptation depends on such factors as sex, genetics, biological age, training age, level of fitness and motivation. Such factors must be considered when establishing the goals of your speed training program.

2. Individualisation

This is where you adjust your training methods to the particular adaptive ability and response of one specific athlete. This has to be done as much as possible in order to get the best results. Biodiversity is a very real, very obvious factor. Giving all your athletes the same generic program to follow will result in the same generic results.

It cannot be emphasised enough that you must individualise your athlete's program. If you are working 1:1 or with small groups, the program is easily tailored to the individual needs. However, the difficulties presented in training the speed of a team of 30, 40 even 50+ athletes and still individualising the program. There are solutions to this that will get into later, but such things as testing, goal setting meetings and organisation are the first steps toward getting the most out of your athletes. Breaking goals and expectations down based on training age, fastest times, strength levels, etc. will produce far greater results than the 'one size fits all' ideology employed in most programs.

3. Overload

Overload can be termed as any training stimulus significant enough to elicit an adaptive response. For athletes to continue to adapt, said stimulus has to be increased along specific lines. The degree of this increased load can be measured by:

— Volume

— Intensity

— Density

— Duration

Volume can be measured by the number of repetitions performed, the total distance run or the total weight lifted. For example: 10x30m = a volume of 300 meters 5 sets of 5 squats at 225 pounds = a volume of 5625 pounds. Intensity is the percent of maximum performance that a particular exercise is performed. An athlete with a personal best in the 100m dash of 11.0 seconds who performs one run at 11.55 seconds equals an intensity of 95%.

Density is the amount of recovery between bouts of exercise, but in relation to the amount of time said exercise takes to complete. An interval workout where an athlete runs for 45 seconds and jogs for 90 seconds is less dense than a workout where the athlete runs for 45 seconds and rests for 45 seconds.

Duration relates to the amount of time the athlete is actually exercising as opposed to recovering from that exercise. A sprinters interval workout of 10x200m may have duration of 5 minutes even though the workout lasts 30+ minutes while a speed workout 6x50m lasting the same length of time may have duration of only 30 - 40 seconds. It is important to consider all these factors and their impact on general adaptation when designing your speed training program.

4. Restoration

Restoration, or recovery, is the aided return of the athlete to his/her normal state through means such as massage, nutrition, hydration, recovery work, rest and relaxation. The term also refers to the amount of time required to go from the fatigued post workout state to the point of super adaptation. For example, it may take 48-72 hours to fully recover from an intense neuromuscular training session. Adaptation takes place not from the workout itself, but from the effectiveness of the recovery mechanisms employed between (in the case of speed development) neuromuscular training days.

5. Reversibility

Also known as 'detraining', this is the loss of adaptation due to either lack of or inadequate training stimulus. How long it takes to start to 'get out of shape' depends on many variables and is of particular concern in track and field athletes during the peaking phase. For example, aerobic enzyme production begins to decrease after just 24 hours. Yet strength may be maintained for several weeks of inactivity, though muscle fibre size will decrease fairly quickly.

Energy System

First, we will briefly look at the energy systems we are working with in our speed development. There are three that we have to be concerned with:

1. ATP/CP System (Adenosine TriPhoshate/Creatine Phosphate)
2. The Anaerobic Lactate (Glycolytic) System
3. Aerobic System

Ultimately these systems describe the metabolic pathways available to replace ATP concentrations. In the glycolytic system, as hydrogen ion concentrations increase, enzyme activity decreases and glucose or glycogen breaks down to pyruvate to provide energy.

To design an effective program, knowledge of your sport/event and how these energy systems affect success in that sport/event is critical to making improvements. The next topic requiring some attention is that of understanding the 4 body systems that must be developed with your training.

The Neuromuscular System

This system consists of the elements of the Central Nervous System that control skeletal muscle activity as well as muscle tissue that is involved in creating force production during athletic performance. The degree of effectiveness of the Central Nervous System is the single greatest factor in performance. Developing the neuromuscular system should be the most important focus of your training. This system must be trained in the absence of fatigue in order to elicit the best results. Despite its importance, this system is widely underdeveloped in most programs.

The Neuroendocrine System

This system operates by releasing hormones into the blood stream during exercise. By having certain hormones in the blood stream, strength development, recovery from workouts and other metabolic functions are significantly enhanced. So certain types of exercise produce clear responses to the endocrine system where effectively designed training can result in marked improvement in performance.

The Musculoskeletal System

This system consists of the muscle tissue responsible for force production, connective tissue and the bones. It is important to note that force created and force applied are not the same. The musculoskeletal system facilitates the transformation of created force to applied force. It is critical to develop postural stability as well as postural alignment in order to enable efficient movement patterns as well as prevent injuries.

The Proprioceptive System

This system's job is to sense and provide the body with information concerning body position, movement, and coordinative abilities. Many movements and actions in speed development, as well as in athletic performance as a whole, are considered reflexive. Thus they are reliant on proprioceptive function. Athletes who can quickly and easily respond to their body position and movement are at a decisive advantage in regards to overall skill development and therefore performance. In order to effectively and efficiently develop this system, athletes must engage in activities that challenge their coordination and balance.

6

Planning and Control of Athletic Training

The start of any movement always sets up the sequence of the kinematic system for the remainder of the lift. There are no exceptions. The beginning predetermines, to a great extent the end result; especially in short duration lifts.

Body Positioning

The amount of time spent on the establishing the start varies from lift to lift. The shorter lifts demand that more attention be devoted to the exact and very precise positioning of the body before even starting the pull from the floor. Longer time events do not seem to require as much concentration on the body positions. However, if the positioning of the feet, limbs and torso are too far out of the proper start posture then the lift will in all likelihood be lost or an injury may result. It can also be said that the longer time that is spent in the exercise, the less the strength component is actually displayed during the lift and the less significance the starting position plays in the final outcome.

V. I Rodionov stated in 1967 that the starting position will affect the barbell trajectory, the force produced by the athlete, the degree to which the muscles are included in the work of moving the weight, the amplitude through which the bar moves and the speed and the execution perfection of the lift. The start, obviously, is an important part of the lift. The start position is a separate phase of every lift and developing the perfect start takes time to perform correctly. It has been noted that normally once the basics of the lift are learned then the athlete will disregard any further start technique improvements. Eventually this particular aspect of the lift is set aside and neglected, leading to possible development of what may be an imperfect beginning. Smart coaches and athletes will set up specific times in the strength program to address the techniques of the start.

Two starts are evident in the lifting world, static and dynamic. In the static start the lifter remains in a motionless position for several seconds before actually pulling on the bar. Active movement before the pull represents the athlete utilising the dynamic pull. A dynamic start position establishes a state of equilibrium between the athlete and the bar. Included in this sequence of events will be the placement of the feet in relationship to the bar, the grip, the width of the grip, the torso angle compared to the floor, the degree of flexion in the back, hips, knees and ankles, and finally the position of the shoulder joint as it relates to the barbell on the floor. Body type will have a bearing on determining the best start position for each lifter.

Checking on the various beginning positions leads to five variations:

1. The upper torso is tipped backward with the shoulders behind the bar as the athlete assumes the start position
2. The athlete lowers into the position by dropping down to where the hamstrings are touching the calf

muscles. After making contact the hips are then raised up in a crisp manner until the athlete reaches a comfortable level at which point the lift begins in earnest

3. The athlete raises and then lowers the hips several times while getting set up and then lifts the bar
4. The athlete addresses the bar by taking a hold of it without bending the knees. After a moment or two the athlete dives to the bar by bending at the knees and while taking advantage of the short, or anticipated short, amortisation phase begins to lift the weight
5. The dive style, which is seldom used by elite lifters, involves approaching the barbell and while taking in a deep breath, quickly bending at the knees and literally 'diving at the bar', and grabbing hold then lifting upward. This is seldom used because the grip or position of the grip is not always as precise as it needs to be.

Experienced lifters generally use the first or the third style to get the bar moving off the floor. The start can be broken down into seventeen parts.

1. The initial approach to the bar
2. The width of the stance at the start
3. Feet position under the bar
4. Stance at the bar
5. The grip width on the bar
6. The grip on the bar
7. Angle of the thigh in relationship the torso
8. The elbow position
9. The torso position
10. Head position

11. Preparing to move the bar
12. Interaction with the bar
13. Shifting of the body links prior to movement of the bar
14. Shoulder and hip joint interaction with the bar
15. The alignment of the shoulder joint to maximise the pull
16. The alignment of the hip joint to maximise the pull
17. The initial pull off the floor

Most novice lifters encounter a number of difficulties when it comes to mastering the elements of the start. Beginning with the mobility of the joints, flexibility issues, problems with keeping the proper arch or a straight back, trying to lift the bar with the arms and not the rest of the body, and trying to accelerate the bar at the immediate instant it breaks from the floor. These are just a few of the reasons one would concentrate on the start variations and each of the attending elements. Each body is built differently, neuromuscularly, psychologically and physiologically. Additional points to be considered are the habits that have previously been formed in earlier training situations and in other sports. These differences have to be taken into account when deciding on the start position.

One may think the approach would not be that big of a deal when lifting the bar off the floor or performing any specific lift but it actually is the beginning of the start. Just consider:

— Is the lifter mentally and physically prepared to lift the weight?

— Are they just physically going through the motions or are they mentally engaged?

— Have they visually, i.e. mentally lifted this in their mind in the past?

— Do they believe this weight can be lifted at this time and under these specific conditions?

It all adds up to either negatively or positively affecting the outcome of the lift.

The width of the stance at the start

The measurement of stance width is fraught with uncertainty as there is no commonly recognised point of reference. It would seem to be a simple matter of measuring between the heels of each foot, inside to inside. But it is not accepted practice so the best advice unless one is using the sumo stance in the dead-lift is to place the feet pelvic width or narrower. Some coaches even say this foot placement should be the width of the palms. Have the athlete get into the recommended position and see how it feels. Slight adjustments may be necessary but unless the sumo is being used it's best to keep the feet closer together as this will maximise the force applied to the barbell. This is particularly true for the Olympic lifts as the reduction in the vertical component will be evident during the movement.

Foot position

Early on many coaches believed that the shins should be touching the bar. It was thought that by doing so the bar would cover the least amount of ground coming up, i.e. in a straight line from floor to finish. But starting out like this tends to crowd the other links in the body so they are not set up into an efficient pulling position. Especially affected is the back. Beginning so close to the bar makes it unlikely the lifter will be able to straighten it out to begin lifting.

Current thinking has the bar positioned nearly on the shins with the exact distance determined by the relative experience of the lifter and their particular body type. For example, a novice should be placing their feet so the shins are approximately 5cm from the bar. The shoulders should be situated in a vertical line with the toes. Advanced lifters will vary slightly from this placement. Positioning the feet here places the barbell at the centre of gravity within the support platform of the body. In other words the bar is being lifted from a powerful starting point by being balanced and supported at the centre of gravity, within the athletes' physical structure.

The stance

There are two standard positions used by the majority of lifters, with tremendous variations applied to each one. The first is with the narrow stance. The lifter places the feet parallel to one another and pointed straight ahead. The second position commonly seen is with the feet angled outward at least 10 to 15 degrees.

If an athlete is setting up in a sumo stance for the dead-lift, the feet will be spaced much wider apart to where they are nearly touching the plates on the bar. The toes in this instance will then be pointing out at an angle approaching 45 degrees. It has been noticed that at the wider angles, the support for the bar is diminished and balance is easily lost either to the front or to the rear.

Determining the angle of the feet to the bar is made by measuring between the long axis of the feet, perpendicular to the bar. In each case of finding the best foot placement angle, the position needs to feel natural and comfortable to the lifter. In some cases this will be determined by the joint mobility of the lifter.

The grip width on the bar

Each lifter will have a favourite grip spot on the bar from which they want to begin the lift. Some go narrow, as the sumo lifters do, and others will have a "wide grip". In the squat a "wide grip" is often necessary in order to get the hands on the bar. The wide grip is the favourite of those with limited shoulder mobility, especially in the squat, but a hold greater than shoulder width will cause grip problems.

Most lifters are better off using the medium to narrow grip positions on the bar. These are, respectively speaking, just outside the knees and just on the inner edge of the knurling on the bar. The Olympic lifters have somewhat of an advantage as their hand spacing is per a formula determined by the width of the shoulders, the length of the arms and the torso. Power-lifters, to my knowledge, have no such formula to guide them in the correct hand placement prior to the lifts; certainly this is true for the squat and the dead-lift.

The grip on the bar

Several methods of gripping the bar are in use today. The normal grip positions are: alternate-one hand overhand with the other underhand, narrow, overhand, overhand thumb less, underhand, and hook style. All of these can be spaced narrow, medium and wide and each one has advantages and disadvantages during the different lifts. If the athlete wants a secure grip, one that keeps the bar in the same plane on both sides then the hook grip is ideal but it requires getting used to. It hurts initially and many lifters, at least in the power-lifting ranks, do not like it. Olympic lifters use it extensively due to the solid grip it provides. The thumb will tire easily during the first few workouts with the hook grip. It is one of the most, if not the most, reliable grip that can be used to lift heavy weights.

Angle of the thigh in relationship to the torso

The thighs have to angle a little outward to remain in line

with the knees and feet. The degree will be reflected in the starting position and the arm drop. In other words the arms should be lightly touching the legs near the thighs and knees during a dead-lift. Squat thigh angle at the beginning will depend on the width of the stance. Ideally, setting up so the lifters centre of gravity is directly in line with the barbells centre of gravity will be the most advantageous in lifting the weight. This is most efficiently accomplished if the thighs are angled to the same degree as the feet in the starting position. Horizontal alignment of the thigh depends on the relationship between the length of the torso and legs. This can vary a great deal between individual lifters due to the flexibility and mobility of the joints making up the lower body.

The elbow position

Most coaches agree that the arms need to be straight at the beginning of the pull. However there is a slight difference of opinion as to whether or not they must be rigid. Some practitioners believe the arms should be viewed as if they were ropes or somewhat relaxed at the start. Others point out the fact that a relaxed state in the arms fails to transfer instant power to the bar at the precise time it is needed to move it off the floor. An optimum amount of arm tension on the bar, at the start is a precursor to a solid grip. An additional benefit of maintaining tight arms is the hands can be cocked inward, thus helping to keep the bar closer to the body.

Thc torso position

This by far is the most important aspect of the entire start process. The overriding consensus is the lower back must be arched or at the very least kept straight. It has been noticed that although keeping the back in this arched position is most common there are some high level athletes who have a slight rounding to their back as they begin the pull.

The vertebrae form the natural link between the upper and lower body parts and if it is not kept rigid the movement loses energy. The requirement of a rigid torso and arched back requires strong tense erector muscles. Keeping an arch in the back is difficult for some trainees to do. According to some literature this is due the fact that an arched back is not a requirement for everyday living so non-lifters or those with little prior experience do not know how it feels. Lack of mobility in the hips can also lead to an inadequate arch.

If that is the case then a few of these exercises may help you develop this area. Before looking over the list, it may be best to remind you that some lifters will simply not be able to get into this favourable back arched position due to their physical peculiarities. If you are one of these, then keep the back as flat as possible.

— Start with a straight back while standing up
— Now squat into the starting position while maintaining the arch
— After the regular session is over add in one to four sets of static hold "good mornings" with a weighted barbell on the back
— Keep a tight arched back for five to fifteen seconds
— Develop the sense of keeping the centre of gravity over the toes to derive the utmost effect from these movements. In doing so the major portion of the load will be on the erector spinae in the lumbar area
— After several sessions of following this sequence the lifter will know what an arch feels like and will keep it intact as they lift.

Head position

Studies have been conducted on the position the head, at the start. Photo analysis at the Olympics found the athletes tilting their heads upwards an average of 30° at the beginning of their lifts. One was even tilted up 42°. Beginners should not be looking at the ceiling as it throws off their balance. Look instead at the recommended 30° angle. By doing so the shoulder girdle is placed in a solid anatomical position. The scapula is pulled back and drawn together and the chest is pushed outward or forward in relationship to the shoulder blades.

Preparing to move the bar

Setting up is not just a simple 'grab the bar and lift' sort of an affair. Instead each element contributes to the successful lift. In this case the essential technique is one of moving the hips down then up into the final static lifting position. Moving the pelvis in the opposite direction i.e. up and then down, forces the muscles to change direction from a yielding to an overcoming effort. The end result is a lower maximum muscular output. It may be easier to remember if you squat into position.

Interaction with the bar

The lifter will be in a static stance at the very instance of putting vertical force to the bar. At the same time this is taking place it is also necessary to make certain optimal tension is present in the muscles and that each of the joints has enough flexibility and mobility to perform the lift.

Being too tense in the muscles or relaxed in any of the kinematic links will be cause for lower power output. Generally the hips will be lower at the static beginning point than during the actual instant of the pull. Keeping the thighs at about ten to twenty degrees above horizontal seems to be the most advantageous. This however, depends on the body type mentioned earlier.

Next month in the final part of this article we will look at shifting of the body links prior to movement of the bar, shoulder and hip joint interaction with the bar, the alignment of the shoulder joint to maximise the pull, the alignment of the hip joint to maximise the pull and the initial pull off the floor .

Shifting of the body links prior to movement of the bar

Many lifters raise their hips and begin to straighten their legs slightly after getting into the static posture at the start of the lift. According to research by Lukashev and Frolovthis is because it takes a few hundredths of a second (0.14-0.16 seconds) for enough force to be generated to actually lift the bar from the floor.

Shoulder and hip joint interaction with the bar

As this is taking place and more force is being applied to the bar then the bar is beginning to bend as it starts upward. The hips continue to go upward until the applied force equals the weight on the bar and all of the body links are synchronised and in position to move the bar off the floor. This is the dynamic posture at the actual start and is the precise moment when the weight leaves the floor.

The alignment of the shoulder joint to maximise the pull

At the initiation of the pull the shoulder joints must be in a position to equally load the body's kinematic links. The shoulders are in a powerful pulling position if they are directly over the bar at the instant the bar separates from the floor. However, this is not consistent with theory or with observations of elite lifters where the best position of the shoulders will be in front of the bar. The reasoning behind this shift forward is that the vertical aspect of the body's structure places the center of gravity at the center of the ankle joints.

It has been found that the elite lifter will automatically place their shoulder joint five to fifteen centimeters in front of the bar at the instant the weight leaves the floor. Again the body type seems to dictate the best distance. Those with short legs and long torsos have an advantage if they stand zero to five centimeters in front of the bar. Six to nine centimeters seems to work very well for those with proportions similar top to bottom. An athlete with long legs and a short upper torso would benefit in placing themselves anywhere from ten to fifteen centimeters in front of the bar.

Now bear in mind these recommendations are for the elite lifters. A novice lifter does not have the necessary structural development to 'pull in' the barbell at the instant the weight leaves the ground. Instead they would be better advised to line up with the shoulder joints in the same line as the bar or just slightly in front of it at the time the bar leaves the floor. Once the lifter has gained muscle mass and experience they should begin to shift toward the correct position in front of the bar. This obviously is an evolving process for each lifter and coach.

The alignment of the hip joint to maximise the pull

If the hips are low at the instant the bar leaves the ground the legs are overloaded relative to the remainder of the body and the upper torso will be under loaded as it straightens up. On the other hand if the hips are high at the instant the bar leaves the ground the torso will be overloaded and the extensor muscles of the thigh will be underutilised in the effort. If both the thigh and the torso muscles are equal in strength then the angle of the thighs and the torso with the floor will be fairly similar. Many novice lifters are stronger in their torso extensors and lift with higher hips. As the athlete gains experience and strength then the legs should catch up with the torso and the angles between the two, i.e. the thigh angle and the back angle, should be approaching the same angular degree.

The initial pull off the floor

When all of the pieces of the lift start are properly in place then each of the links in the power chain will be at their most advantageous position to produce the maximum power. Correct positioning means that each link will be loaded in a uniform manner and contributing their utmost to a successful lift.

The dynamic start is the precise moment when the lifter and the barbell are equalised and become a single unit in relation to the base of support. By keeping the heels on the ground helps to maintain the horizontal to shin angle alignment which in turn helps to keep the back arched which translates to less force having to be generated by the legs.

Strength Training and the Young Athlete

Where do we start?

To start, there are definitive differences between adolescent boys and adolescent girls with respect to strength and strength production. In boys, absolute muscular strength grows consistently between the ages of 7 to 19. In girls, strength gains are incurred on a consistent level until about the age of 15, when a period of stagnation occurs and a strength gain plateau. By the end of the pubescent ages boys are roughly 50% stronger than girls.

Factors to Consider

There are several factors to consider when programming strength training for young athletes:

— *Central Nervous System Maturity* - The true argument with respect to children and weight lifting should not be based on the maturity of the child's muscular system, but rather the advancement of the child's central nervous system (CNS). Within proper application of load, volume and intensity, a child's muscular system will not be compromised by weight training activities. However, a lack of motor control (a function of the CNS) will affect the child's ability to perform weight-training exercises safely. It is therefore the maturity of the CNS that is the ultimate determining factor.

— *Cross Section Of Muscle* - A larger muscle infers a greater strength potential. While hypertrophy of this sort is not hormonally possible with pre-adolescent athletes, this fact is why I advocate that early adolescent athletes train with hypertrophy-based responses in mind.

— *Biological Maturity* - Biological age, unlike a child's chronological age, is not actually visible. Biological age is based in large part to the physiological development of the various organs and systems in the body. The adequate development of bone and the efficiency of the heart and lungs to transport oxygen are examples of items that comprise biological age. These become important when determining the volume or intensity of the training program for the young athlete.

— *Hormonal Issues* - Androgenic hormones are low in pre-adolescent athletes. This means that hypertrophy-based responses are all but impossible but strength gains are however, very possible.

— Technical Issues - Providing a proper foundation of the technical merits of strength training is paramount when working with youngsters.

The arguments for and against

On the argument of effectiveness, adequately programmed strength training has shown considerable positive effects with regards to pre-adolescents. In terms of danger or contraindication, the greatest concern lies in ligament or bone damage. Elastic, young skeletons and connective tissue can be injured if loads are excessive. This is why loads must be kept low and proper form strictly followed. Of interesting note is the argument regarding strength training and stunted growth. In the event of bone or growth plate damage growth can in fact be stunted. But, if proper strength training parameters are prescribed, than the opposite is true. Muscle pull, is a significant factor that stimulates bone thickness. More over, 'intermittent use of submaximal resistance stimulates height growth'.

Assessment is essential

One keynote point that have preached endlessly is the fact that an orthopaedic assessment MUST precede any strength training prescription. Postural defects can be made worse by incorrect application of strength training, and conversely improved by correct application. An assessment is a mandatory pre-cursor to any child-based strength-training program.

Exercises for young athletes

Here is a list of exercises, adopted from, to use with young athletes. The exercises in this list get progressively more difficult. Start younger athletes on the earlier exercises and progress them systematically over the years.

- — Obstacle courses, rope pulling, climbing
- — Vertical strength (standing push-ups), hanging exercises
- — Bodyweight exercises and medicine ball based activities/throws
- — Horizontal strength (push-ups, pull-ups)
- — Dumbbell & barbell exercises
- — Single leg squats, dead lifts, step-ups, good mornings

Strength and Muscle Balance Checks

A speed strength imbalance between two opposing muscle groups may be a limiting factor in the development of speed. Muscle balance testing to compare the strength of opposing muscle groups is important to prevent injury and guarantee maximum speed of muscle contraction and relaxation. Muscle imbalance can slow you down and result in injury.

Strength Checks

Leg press/body weight ratio

Your leg strength/body weight ratio indicates how easily you can get and keep your body moving at high speeds. This ratio is important to speed improvements in short distances. A good ratio is 2.5:1 or a leg press score two and half times your body weight. If it is less than 2.5 then you should consider modifying the programme to develop leg strength.

Leg strength test

The squat is considered the most functional leg strength test in predicting sprinting and jumping ability. Good 1RM (one rep max) scores are :

— Male athletes 2 x "Body Weight"

— Female athletes 1.5 x "Body Weight"

Hamstring/Quadriceps strength

For each leg record the 1RM for the leg curl and leg extension exercises. Divide your leg curl score by the leg extension score to find the ratio for each leg. For each leg the curl score should be at least 80% of your extension score. If the score is less than 80% then you need to devote more training attention to the hamstrings. To reduce the chance of injury the ratio should be at least 75%.

Bench press

This is a test for upper body strength. The need for maximum upper body strength varies between sports and so it does not always need to be tested for. Good 1RM scores are :

— Male athletes 1.25 x "Body Weight"

— Female athletes 0.8 x "Body Weight"

Balance checks

For each of the following exercise the right and left limb 1RM scores should not differ by more than 10%.

— Hamstrings (leg extension)

— Quadriceps (leg curl)

— Arm Curl

— One arm military press

— Single leg press

The following table are say that values for joint agonist-antagonist ratios at slow isokinetic speeds.

Joint	*Movement*	*Ratio*
Ankle	Plantar flexion/dorsi flexion	3:1
Ankle	Inversion/eversion	1:1
Leg	Extension/flexion	3:2
Hip	Extension/flexion	1:1
Shoulder	Flexion/extension	2:3
Elbow	Flexion/extension	1:1
Lumbar	Flexion/extension	1:1

Where there is an imbalance then you need to devote more training attention to the muscle group of the weaker limb.

Ladder Training

Many muscular endurance and conditioning workouts require high volumes of work which, for neophytes and the de-conditioned achieving these numbers, may seem like a very distant goal. How do you go from only being able to perform a couple of press ups or dips to completing the 100 reps required by some coaches or workouts?

Strength training, like gymnastic training, is part physiological adaptation and part neurological adaptation - by which I mean in many cases the limiting factor, is not the size of your muscles but the nervous supply to those muscles. As strength training is in part a skill, we need to perform repeated movements with sufficient volume to allow the body to learn how to perform the exercises in a skillful coordinated way. Here in lies the problem - the best was to get better at pull ups is to do lots of them, but if you cannot do many in the first place, how do you achieve sufficient volume to get really good at the exercise? Luckily, the conundrum has a solution - and that solution is called "ladder training".

In a normal workout, our neophyte trainee may manage for example an initial set of 7 pull ups, a second set of 5 and a final set of 3 to give him/her a total workout volume of 15 reps. More volume is required to improve the skill of the pull up but insufficient strength makes this a difficult task.

In many strength training circles this principle of repeated efforts to improve specific exercise performance is called "greasing the groove". By applying ladder training to our trainees pull ups, our newbie will be doing more volume and therefore more practice and soon be on their way to improving their pull up numbers to a level which was previously an impossible dream!

Ladder training protocol

— Perform 1 rep of the given exercise

— Rest a few seconds

— Perform 2 reps of the given exercise

— Rest a few seconds

— Perform 3 reps of the given exercise

— Rest a few seconds

— Perform 4 reps of given exercise

— Rest a few seconds etc.

Keep adding one rep and resting a few seconds until you are unable to continue i.e. you mange 5 reps, rest a few seconds but cannot then manage 6. This is the end of the first set. Using our previous trainee as an example again, our beginner client manages to ladder up to 5 reps in the first set - giving a rep total for that set of 15.

After 90 seconds rest, they perform ladders again and reach a high of 4 reps - giving a rep total of 10 reps and on their final set managed 3 reps giving a rep total for that set of 6 reps.

So, in total, our trainee will have completed 31 reps of pull ups - 16 reps more than they could normally have achieved! Ladder training is an excellent tool for increasing overall training volume which can be applied to pretty much any exercise and provides a great way of exposing the trainee to a much higher volume of work than would normally be possible training in a more traditional way. It works very well with "easy" exercises like bodyweight pull ups, press ups and dips, as well as with traditional resistance exercises like squats, bench press and dead lifts - particularly when utilising a substantial load.

Strength Training for Women

A survey of US schoolchildren in 1985 comprising various motor tests showed that the average 18 year old girl could perform only one pull-up. It also showed that the sit up in one minute score peaked for girls at 14 years, with abdominal strength endurance declining from then on. The standing long jump test also indicated that on average girls peak at 14 years. In comparison, the average boy scored significantly higher on the test and improved until 18 years old.

These statistics merely illustrate what everyone knows, that women naturally develop less strength than men. The differences can be explained by the fact that at puberty boys have increased testosterone levels which promotes muscle development and bone growth over the next few years, whereas girls have increased oestrogen which promotes quite fast pelvic bone growth and fat storage around the hips and thighs.

After puberty, boys' relative fat mass decreases from 16 to 13%, while girls' relative fat mass increases from 18 to 26%. Indeed, research has shown that most of the differences in strength between men and women can be explained in terms of differences in lean body mass and muscle and fat distribution. Women have smaller arm girth and greater arm skin fold thickness than men, similar leg girth but greater leg skin fold thickness than men. This different distribution of extra fat and smaller muscle mass accounts for much of the disparity in strength between the sexes, women being about 66 to 75% as strong in the legs and 50 to 60% as strong in the arms.

Nevertheless, research has shown that normalising for lean body mass, which takes out the overall differences in muscle and fat, muscle pound to muscle pound women are similar in strength to men.

Can women respond to strength training?

In the past, it was believed that strength training was unsuitable for women because they were "incapable" of improving their strength. But more recent research has put paid to this theory. Professor Jack Wilmore from the University of Texas showed that after a 10 week training programme women showed a 29% improvement on the bench press and 30% improvement on the leg press, compared to a 17% and 26% improvement from men.

However, while the men showed hypertrophy in the leg and arm muscles, the women did not. Wilmore hypothesised that the reason for the increased strength in women must be due to an increased ability to recruit muscle fibres and coordinate the movements. Later research has shown that women can increase muscle mass significantly. The tentative conclusion must be that in general most women find it more difficult to gain muscle mass. Recently an official summary of all the research regarding strength training for women was presented in the US by the Women's Committee of the National Strength and Conditioning Association. They say that:

1. Women improve fitness, athletic performance and reduce injuries through strength training, just as men do
2. Physiological responses of males and females to the use of weight training and resistance exercise are similar
3. Women should train for strength using the same exercises and techniques as men
4. There is no significant difference between the sexes in the ability to generate force per unit of cross-sectional muscle. Men display greater absolute strength than women largely because they have a greater body size and higher lean body mass to fat ratio
5. Women do experience muscle hypertrophy in response to resistance exercise, but the absolute degree is smaller than in men. The conclusion to be drawn is that women are equally as strength trainable as men. If female athletes want to achieve elite performances they must ensure that comprehensive strength training is fully covered in their training schedules. Competitions, unlike laboratory research, do not compensate for lean body mass. It is the fastest who wins, and that is the end of it. If you want to be that winner, you have to optimise your strength.

What sort of training?

That being said, the next question is, what is the best form of strength training for women? The answer is not a matter of gender but more a matter of the particular requirements of the athlete's event, being the same for both men and women. Looked at from this point of view, any athlete must improve her (or his) strength if their profile is less than the strength demands of their event.

To devise the best strength programme based on the event's requirements, we have to analyse the event in terms of muscle use, the type of contractions each muscle uses, the biomechanics of the movement and whether maximum strength or strength endurance is the goal. This kind of "needs analysis" should govern the design of any strength programme. As an illustration of such an analysis, let us look at running the 10K

In the 10K event, the major leg muscles all work dynamically, such as the quadriceps, the hamstrings, gluteus maximus, hip flexors, calf and dorsi flexors. All these muscles are active at some point during the gait cycle and so it makes sense to strengthen them. However, they must all be strengthened in the right way to maximise 10K performance and injury prevention.

In 10K running 97% of the energy for muscle contractions comes from aerobic metabolism. Thus the predominant muscle fibre units recruited at 10K pace will be the aerobic Type 1 and 2a units. The more anaerobic Type 2a and 2b units may only be recruited towards the end of the race as the muscles tire and glycogen is depleted.

For this reason, the 10K strength programme must have a strength endurance emphasis which targets mainly the Type 1 and Type 2a fibre units. It has been shown that strength athletes who perform a few sets of a few repetitions of very heavy weights e.g. four sets of five reps, have selective hypertrophy in the Type 2b fibres, which would not necessarily benefit the 10k runner, whereas bodybuilders who perform higher volumes of lighter weights e.g. six sets of 12 reps, show hypertrophy in the whole range of muscle fibres.

Although 10K athletes do not want to start bodybuilding, it could be argued that for the leg muscles a strength endurance training programme of high repetitions and lighter weights would be the most suitable for a 10K athlete since the Type 1 and 2a fibres will be targeted effectively. To improve strength endurance, 3 to 5 sets of 12 to 20 repetitions with 45 second rest periods are recommended.

The choice of leg exercises must reflect the biomechanics involved in the running movement. For example, since most thigh muscle activity occurs when one foot is in contact with the ground, single legged exercises with the foot in contact with the ground or equipment will be most relevant. Single legged leg press, lunges or one legged squats are all exercises of this nature which target the muscles in the thigh and bum areas. The range of movement of the joints is also relevant.

For example, as the foot strikes the ground, the knee joint is slightly bent (about 20°). Then the knee flexes to absorb the impact (to around 40°) and then extends again before toe off. The quadriceps muscles act to control the shock absorbing knee flexion movement. Certain strength exercises should be chosen to focus on this range of movement e.g. limited range leg press, especially to help prevent the anterior knee pain which women are prone to because of a greater femur Q angle causing more inward rotation of the knee.

Do not overlook the trunk and hips

The other major body part that requires strength training for running is the trunk and hip area. Here the major muscles involved during running are the erector spinae (back), abdominals (stomach), obliques (side) and abductors (top of the bum). These muscles are not so obviously involved with running as the leg muscles, yet nonetheless serve a very important role in pelvis and trunk stabilisation and posture control. Biomechanical research has shown that for the legs to work effectively in propelling the body, the pelvis and trunk area must be rigid and supported by its muscles, otherwise the drive from the legs will be wasted.

These hip and trunk muscles must also be trained for strength endurance, for similar reasons. However, since they do not work as dynamically as the leg muscles, the exercises chosen should reflect their more static, supporting role. These muscles are best trained with a combination of isometric or static exercises and slow, controlled dynamic exercises of small, specific range.

Lying on one's front over the end of a bench and extending the arms out into a Superman position and maintaining it is an isometric exercise for the back muscles. Three sets of 10 x 10 seconds holding a straight line from the back to the hands will help maintain an upright posture as the muscles must hold the back and shoulder girdle in a rigid extended position.

An example of a slow and controlled exercise which targets a small range is the reverse curl or reverse crunch exercise for the stomach. This involves lying on one's back with legs fully bent. Then, raise the hips an inch off the floor by pulling with the lower abdominals and lower again, keeping the legs completely still. Here the abdominal muscles have to work continually to raise the pelvis and then lower it again, even though it is a small range of movement. This kind of exercise is more relevant to posture control than the more conventional sit up. After all, when we run we keep our upper bodies still, so being very strong at flexing the trunk forwards is not necessarily related to efficient running.

In general, the hip and trunk muscles must be trained for strength endurance using static exercises and exercises with specific ranges of movement for posture control. The choice of exercises must reflect the need to maintain a rigid back with a level pelvis to be able to push off with the legs. Balanced strength in this area also helps prevent lower back and hamstring injuries. In my opinion, the trunk and hip area is very important for 10K strength training programs. Strong legs will only do so much if the trunk is not a well supported, rigid structure. Would a motor racing team put a Formula engine in a car with a Formula 3 chassis?

Training the upper body

To complete the strength analysis, we must consider the upper body. This area is less important for 10K running, but for an all body, balanced strength programme some upper body exercises should be included. Upper body strength will also help with posture and an effective, easy arm action.

A practical way to train the upper body without devoting too much time to it would be to cover most of the major upper body muscles in two or three exercises e.g. seated row together with bench press, or pull-ups together with dips, would target most of the chest, shoulder, upper back and arm muscles.

To summarise the strength training programme for the 10K, all the major muscles involved in running need to be trained with a strength endurance emphasis. The exercises chosen also need to be biomechanically relevant in terms of movement, single legged and foot fixed, and any important joint ranges of movement. This will improve the power and efficiency of running action and help reduce knee injury risks. Training the trunk muscles for endurance, using static and postural specific exercises will increase efficiency by improving the rigidity and support of the trunk. It will also help reduce low back and hamstring injury risks. Exercises covering the upper body muscles will complete a balanced strength programme that is specifically targeted to the athlete's event.

This kind of analysis can be done for any event or sport. First, the correct muscles and movements have to be pinpointed and the role they play in the sport determined. From this the relevant strength training exercise protocols can be designed for the muscles involved. Women athletes should definitely use this method as the starting point for their essential strength training requirements.

Stair Climbing for Lower Body Strength

The first way to improve lower body strength in stair-workouts is to climb every other step. Because doing this puts your legs in a mechanical disadvantage, your muscles have to get stronger to overcome this disadvantage. But this is usually left to very tall athletes or athletes with very long legs. Two steps is usually enough to challenge most anyone. For the purpose of strength improvement it is only necessary to do 1 to 5 sets of 1 to 30 repetitions on each leg. You can either alternate or use 1 leg at a time.

Lower body

A lower body strength workout can look something like this:

- Round 1
  - Walk up 20 flights
  - Stretch when you reach the top
  - Take the elevator down
- Round 2
  - Do 30 stair-lunges: 15 on weaker side followed by 15 on your stronger side
  - Climb 2 steps each lunge
- Round 3

  - Do 30 stair-lunges in alternating fashion
  - Climb 2 steps each lunge
- Round 4
  - Do 30 crossover-lunges in alternating fashion
  - Climb 1 step for each lunge and over time progress to 2 steps for each lung
- Round 5
  - Do 30 crossover lunges from side: 15 on weaker side then 15 on your stronger side
  - Climb 1 step for each lunge and over time progress to 2 steps for each lung
- Round 6
  - Do 30 side to side lunges in alternating fashion
  - Climb 1 step for each lunge and over time progress to 2 steps for each lung
- Round 7
  - Do 30 side step ups: 15 on weaker side followed by 15 on your stronger side
  - Climb 1 step for each lunge and over time progress to 2 steps for each lung

As your strength improves you have many options to challenge you further. Possible options are:

- Use dumbbells or barbell
- Use a weighted vest
- Reduce your rest intervals between sets
- Increase your sets (rounds)

Address frontal and transverse movements In this workout you will be doing lunges in all planes of motion. Remember that it is very important to address frontal (side to side) and transverse (rotational) planes because that is where many athletes are weakest and is probably why athletes get hurt in those planes so frequently. We usually do not address these planes in our exercise routines but constantly use these planes in our everyday lives

Trainer's Perspective

We dissected the technique of performing a full squat in Successful Coaching Issue 21- The King of exercises: the Squat. In this issue, we are going to describe what the coach should be looking at while the lifter is under the bar. The task of the coach is to be constantly aware of the proper mechanics of the squat and then 'cueing' the lifter to perform them in the right manner to make progress and to avoid injury.

Programming

In order to be 'technically' correct and successful, the athlete has to develop engram patterns very precisely during the early developmental stages of the learning curve. By definition, an engram is a neuromuscular, subconscious pathway of performing a physical movement. Superior exercise adeptness occurs from repeating this training process. At the top level of training the mind no longer consciously dwells on the exercise movement, instead the elite lifter is able to focus on the shear muscle energy necessary to move the weight. Thus, the move is ingrained in the subconscious and automatic. Can you envision yourself stepping out from the rack with a six hundred pound barbell and then having to decide if you needed to first move your hips back or bend your knees to begin the lift.

A well-trained coach will effectively assist the athlete performing the exercise by providing both verbal and visual cues as to how best to perform the move. Improvements in technique will be seen in most lifters if the coach pays attention to the details of the lift and provides meaningful feedback. This means the coach has to observe the athlete from a 360 degree perspective. Videotape is an excellent motivator, as the lifter will clearly recognise errors of form, especially with the coach reviewing the tape with them. The coach must always keep in mind one important aspect:

— Is the movement under total control?

If the load is not completely under control, all of attending spotters must take prompt action to protect the lifter from harm. The coach will have to pay close attention to these three major safety points:

— Telling the spotters to assist in re-racking the bar if they are not aware of the lifters predicament

— Lowering the weight on the bar so the exercise may be completed correctly the next repetition

— Making certain the athlete gets additional rest time before trying the next set.

Coaching points

Observation from the front vantage point at the beginning of the lift:

— Has the lifter centered the bar firmly on the back and shoulders

— Is the lifter in an upright standing position and not leaning over- the bar placement will dictate this portion of the stance. The low bar position causes the athlete to bend forward in order to keep the bar centered over the balance point of their body

— Is the chest held high at the beginning of the lift

— Is the head flexed forward or extended slightly upward, but not looking at the ceiling

— Is the bar properly situated and secure on the back, i.e. not dropping downward

— Is the back neutral to slightly arched and in a braced position

— Is the lifter standing straight and tall and not tilted to either one side or the other

— Remind the lifter to abdominal brace.

Start of the lift from the rear observation point

— Is the bar symmetrically loaded with the correct weight on both ends

— Are the collars securely attached to both sides

— Is the bar correctly positioned, spaced and resting on the shoulders/upper back at the correct height for the athlete

— Are the lifters hands in the positioned properly and placed evenly on the bar

— Has the lifter placed their body under the bar and are they in the correct position to lift the bar off the hooks

— Has the head remained correctly in line with the back and not flexed forward

— Is the back rigid, slightly arched and braced.

Start of the lift as seen from the right side

— Are the feet aligned evenly and not forward or backward relative to one another

— Is the athlete standing tall

— Have the hips started the rearward movement, or have the knees started bending first

— Is the back staying straight and solid

— Has the head stayed in line with the back in a neutral position or is it slightly extended.

The two-three steps back and the initial set up as observed from the front of the lifter

— Is the chest still kept high
— Have the two to three steps to the rear been small enough to clear the rack pins
— Is the body still vertically aligned or has it twisted off to either side
— Is there movement in the hips as the bar set up is competed
— Has the movement been stabilised and did it stop
— Are the feet spaced at lest shoulder width or wider
— Are the toes angled outward and remaining in line with the knees.

The back out and set up as seen from the rear

— Is the movement still under control by the lifter
— Is the back still solid and in a slightly arched position
— Are the hips starting to move from side to side in a continuing effort to balance the weight load
— Are the feet moving around or are they steady and sticking to one place on the platform
— Is the bar steady on the shoulders or is it moving around instead of being held firmly in place.

The back out and set up as viewed from the athlete's side

— Are the back out steps under control
— Is the athlete standing tall under the load
— Are the feet correctly positioned in relative to one another and front to rear
— Is the back solid, slightly arched and braced.

The descent as observed directly in front of the lifter

— Is the head lined up with the back

— Is the head positioned correctly and not tipped off to one side

— Are the hips even or are they moving to the side

— Are the feet in the correct position and in line with one another

— Did the hips move backward before the knees started to flex.

The descent as seen from the rear

— Are the hips coming backward towards you before movement seen or felt any where else

— Is the back staying braced, solid and slightly arched

— Are the lower legs remaining perpendicular to the floor

— Is the head still in the upright position and not tilted to one side.

The descent observed from the sides

— Did the hips move backward before any other movement was started

— Is the back staying braced, solid and slightly arched

— Is the head being kept line with the back or slightly angled upward 10 to 20 degrees

— Is the load centered in the middle and slightly to rear of the feet

— Is the body tilting forward to any great extent

— Does the bar move downward in a straight line: there should be very little movement fore and aft of this imaginary vertical line

— Is this imaginary bar path appearing to go from down the ears to the middle of the feet
— Has the lifter accelerated the bar toward the bottom of the move
— Is the upper body angle in relation to the floor remaining the same throughout the descent phase of the lift
— Are the heels firmly in contact with the floor.

The bottom position as seen from the front

— Is the head in line with the rest of the body
— Is the bar still placed evenly on the shoulders
— Has the body remained square with the lifting platform or has the athlete started to tip toward one side
— Has the body continued to face the front of the rack or lifting platform or have they twisted to one side
— Are the knees still aligned over the feet.

The bottom position viewed from behind the athlete

— Is the back appearing to remain tight, slightly arched and braced or has it flexed at the bottom
— Is the bar even on the body from side to side or has it shifted to one side
— Has the body tilted to one side
— Is the athlete twisting to one side or the other.

The bottom position-viewed from the sides of the athlete

— Is the back rigid, slightly arched and braced
— Is the chest still out
— Is the head parallel to the floor or extended slightly at 10 to 20 degrees

— Are the lower legs close to perpendicular with the floor
— Is the angle of the back and joint hip similar to those of the knees/lower legs
— Is the body slanted to one side or the other
— Has the body twisted to one side
— Are the heels remaining in contact with the floor.

The ascent as seen from the front

— Did the initial upward move begin with the head and chest starting upward
— Did you notice the hands beginning with an upward push on the bar
— Is the torso angle staying the same throughout the upward phase
— Is the body positioned straight to the front
— Has it tipped to one side
— Has it twisted on the long axis
— Did the body tilt forward
— Is the head still stable and at the correct angle
— Were the legs and body moving from side to side.

Viewing the ascent from the rear

— Did the first upward move start with the chest, head and arms
— Did the body shift backward during the first move up
— Did the buttocks rise before the head, chest and arms moved upward
— Did the buttocks move laterally
— Is the bar moving evenly upward without a windmill side to side sway

— Is the loaded bar staying in line with the rack and not twisting to one side or the other.

Why you need E-Lifts in your Training Plan

If you have been in the gym during the past few years, you have probably heard these strength training strategies tossed around; light weight / high reps and heavy weight / low reps. The newest strength training strategy on the block is Slow Reps, which refers to a slow moving weight lifting tempo. New training techniques can be positive, particularly if they evolve from an established and proven system of training. Plyometrics is a good example of the positive evolution of training methods.

Plyometrics take different forms, but these exercises are closely related to calisthenics that were used by coaches and drill sergeants during the 40s - 70s. Then some Russian engineers took calisthenics, applied some basic science for sports specific training, and evolved this form of exercise to a new level.

Today we call these exercises plyometrics. Coaches use plyometrics worldwide to improve athletic performance by developing fast-twitch muscle fiber. The evolution of plyometrics teaches us that it s important to challenge training methods and improve them when possible. On the positive side, the Slow Reps method reinforces the need to isolate muscle groups during strength training. Since Arthur Jones and Dr. Ellington Dardin hit the training scene in the 70s with their versions of high-intensity training (HIT), the principle of isolation has been one of the three key concepts in my strength-training programs.

Isolation means to train one muscle group completely by eliminating other groups that attempt to jump in and assist the targeted muscle group once those muscles get fatigued. This allows the muscle group to get more work, and the targeted muscles adapt to this training method by becoming bigger and stronger. Isolation is an important training strategy and the Slow Reps method clearly helps to isolate targeted muscle groups. And that is positive, but Slow Reps can be limiting because muscles adapt. You cannot be around an exercise physiologist very long without hearing the word "adaptation," because that is what muscles do. When muscles are trained, they adapt. Training slow develops slow-twitch muscle fiber, but it is necessary to train fast to reach fast-twitch fiber.

Slow reps, as well as the traditional lifting tempo of up-on-two and down-on-four, works slow muscle fiber. Again, that is positive because slow-twitch fiber is close to half of your muscle fiber, but that leaves you with the other half of your muscle fiber decreasing in size and strength. Now, if you plan living life in slow motion, or play a sport where being slow is positive, then you may not want to add E-lifts to your training program. But if you want to work all of your muscle fiber, then just try E-lifts one time, and you will know that this method is the real deal.

Why you need to work all muscle fiber types

There can be swings in muscle fiber composition, but essentially, we all have three types of muscle fiber that need to be trained. The fast-twitch muscle actually has two types of fiber — fast and super-fast. The fast muscle moves 5 times faster than the slow muscle, and the super-fast moves 10 times faster than the slow muscle fiber. The following chart shows that while there are differences in muscle fiber composition, muscle types can be developed based on the way they are trained.

Muscle fiber type	*Average person*	*Sprint trained*	*Aerobic trained*
Slow (type I)	40%	40%	55%
Fast (IIa)	50%	20%	40%
Super-fast (IIx)	10%	40%	5%

Sprinters, who train fast, have higher percentages of the super-fast (IIx). Endurance trained individuals, who train slow, have more slow muscle fiber (type I). While we are born with slightly different muscle composition, the point is; super-fast muscle can be developed, if it is trained correctly. And E-Lifts do the job. Since we live life in-motion at varying rates of speed, and most sports movements are dynamic (if not ballistic), E-Lifts, therefore, offers a more functional strength development method for sports applications and life in general.

E-Lifts for professional Athletes and older adults

There are many new studies that show explosive lifting to be more effective than traditional lifting: Professional athletes use explosives types of lifting because Olympic lifts are proven to yield better results in power than traditional power lifting. Researchers show that 88 percent of US professional football coaches use Olympic lifting in their training and 94% use plyometric drills.

The reason so many professional teams use explosive techniques in their strength training programs is simple, superior results and a complete body of research showing that E-Lifting yields better results in performance.

E-Lifts are clearly superior for athletes, but what about the rest of us? E-Lifts again outperform other training methods. In a major new study, researchers show that older adults respond better to rapid-rate-of-force movements, and this type of training can be performed safely even at older ages.

Progressive resistance training that incorporates rapid rate-of-force development movements may be safely undertaken in healthy older adults and results in significant gains in muscle strength, muscle power, and physical performance. Such improvements could prolong functional independence and improve the quality of life.

A new, landmark study shows that explosive lifting is the most successful training strategy for older adults: Therefore, using heavy loads during explosive resistance training may be the most effective strategy to achieve simultaneous improvements in muscle strength, power, and endurance in older adults.

We are not talking about using light weight and moving through a set with a lot of quick up-and-down (fast) repetitions. We are talking about using heavy weight with explosion during the movements away from the centre of the body. There is a big difference in performing repetitions quickly as opposed to explosively.

E-Lifting Mechanics

E-Lifts is short for the explosive technique and is an attempt to take the best from the world of Olympic Lifting — Clean and Jerk, Snatch — and the best from traditional lifting techniques used by bodybuilders and fitness trainers. Simply adding an explosive movement on all push and press exercises will accomplish the fast-fiber training goal, which means you are working more muscle fiber than with slow movements. That is why E-Lifting yields better results. Train fast to get fast, train slow and you are only using the slow muscle fiber.

Exercises performed as a push or a press type of exercise are connected to muscle groups loaded with fast-twitch fiber. And these muscle groups require a fast, explosive tempo when pushing the resistance away from the body in order to reach the fast fiber. Examples of exercises would be bench press or any chest press type of machine, leg press, shoulder press, and even calf raises qualify as a push type of exercise.

E-Lifting involves a brief, 1- to 2-second pause at the bottom of a lifting exercise. This will fully stretch the muscle and perhaps make the Slow Reps fans feel more comfortable with the technique. Then push the resistance with explosive thrust away from the body. The down movement prior to the explosive thrust should be similar to the traditional weightlifting tempo of a 2 to 4-second pace. For safety, there are two key points. There should be a warm-up set performed using the traditional lifting tempo of up-on-two, down-on-four. And you should fully extend the repetition all the way out on the push away from the body, but stop the explosive pushing at the 90% point to avoid injury to the elbows or knees. You don not stop at 90%, just stop pushing at 90% and fully extend.

When visiting a gym one will find many an athlete doing all sorts of exercises with all sorts of reps and sets. The question is why are you going to the gym and why are you doing resistance training? When power is your goal, training should be as follows:

Training goal	*Load*	*Reps*	*Sets*	*Rest Between Sets*
1 rep	80-90%	1 - 2	3 - 5	2 - 3 min
Multiple rep	75-85%	3 - 5	3 - 5	2 - 4 min

Many athletes train by rushing the program. This is pointless as it takes 2 to 5 minutes for the neural system to recover from what has just been done. Power training and speed training depends greatly on optimal neural recruitment for maximal performance. Therefore you would train maximally by working according to the recovery time. If you rest less than the 2 minutes the session will become just another endurance or hypertrophy session and little power gains will be made.

Training for power means taxing the neuromuscular system, and with the prescribed rest, the system will have recovered sufficient to perform another 'fast' action. Remember it important to have a fast action. Therefore make sure the weights that you choose allow you to move it fast. Moving a lighter weight 0.5 sec faster, than a 10kg heavier weight 0.5 sec slower will result in less power developed. Refer to the rationale.

The power exercises

These exercises are often referred to as the explosive, core or total body exercises. Muscles involved are the following: gluteals, hamstrings, quadriceps, hip flexors, core area muscles, calves, shoulders, upper shoulder, upper back and upper arms.

1. Clean (power clean or hang clean)
2. Snatch
3. Push press or push jerk
4. ½ squat

These are by far the most explosive exercises an athlete could do in the gym.

Squat and vertical jump

After completing a set of 3 to 5 reps of half squats, immediately do 1 to 3 reps of tuck jumps or vertical jumps. This can also be done with lunge jumps with weights followed by lunge jumps without weights.

Bench press throw

With this exercise make sure you have two spotters, one on each side of the bar. Choose a weight of between 30 to 50% 1RM. Lower the bar and push it back up by exploding with it and try to throw it and with the help of the spotters catch it again. This is a very dangerous exercise but very effective. If uncertain, do the bench press followed by a plyometric push up or do a few medicine ball throws.

The secret of power training in the gym is not to move big weights but rather the speed of movement with lighter weights. Consider the following:

Power is all about Watt output. So if you are a female athlete weighing 60kg, and you lift a 30kg weight into a snatch end position of 1.95m up from the ground in time of 6.2 sec and your doing 3 reps. Your Watt output will be calculated as follows: Determine the weight of the bar in Newtons.

— Weight = 9.8m/s^2 X 30kg = 294 N

— Work = 294 N X 1.95m X 3 = 1719.9 J (1720 J)

— Power = 1720J / 6.2 sec = 277 Watt output

Now consider the same athlete doing the same exercise but using a weight of 40kg x 3 reps in a time of 9.5 sec.

— Weight = 9.8m/s^2 X 40kg = 392 N

— Work = 392N X 1.95M X 3 = 2293 J

— Power = 2293 J / 9.5 sec = 241 Watt output.

If however you could lift the 40kg in less time your Watt output will improve and thus you power. In physics, power is precisely defined as 'the time rate of doing work'. Although the word strength is often associated with slow speeds and power with high speeds of movement, both reflect the ability to exert force at a given speed. Science tells us exactly how to train for power.

7

Nutrition Planning

For every physical activity the body requires energy and the amount depends on the duration and type of activity. Energy is obtained from the body stores or the food we eat. Glycogen is the main source of fuel used by the muscles to enable you to undertake both aerobic and anaerobic exercise. If you train with low glycogen stores you will feel constantly tired, training performance will be lower and you will be more prone to injury and illness. Energy is measured in calories and a calorie (cal) is the amount of heat energy required to raise the temperature of 1g of water 1°C from 14° to 15°C. A kilocalorie (kcal) is the amount of heat required to raise the temperature of 1000g of water 1°C.

Nutrient Balance

Carefully planned nutrition must provide an energy and nutrient balance. The nutrients are:

— *Proteins* - essential to growth and repair of muscle and other body tissues

— *Fats* - one source of energy and important in relation to fat soluble vitamins

— *Carbohydrates* - our main source of energy

— *Minerals* - those inorganic elements occurring in the body and which are critical to its normal functions

— *Vitamins* - water and fat soluble vitamins play important roles in many chemical processes in the body

— *Water* - essential to normal body function - as a vehicle for carrying other nutrients and because 60% of the human body is water

— *Roughage* - the fibrous indigestible portion of our diet essential to health of the digestive system.

Daily energy requirements

Personal energy requirement = basic energy requirements + extra energy requirements Basic energy requirements For every Kg of body weight approximately 1.3 kcal is required every hour. (An athlete weighing 50Kg would require 1.3 x 24hrs x 50Kg=1560 kcal/day)

Extra energy requirements

For each hours training you require approximately 8.5 kcal for each Kg of body weight. (For a two hour training session our 50Kg athlete would require 8.5 x 2hrs x 50Kg=850 kcal) An athlete weighing 50Kg, who trains for two hours, would require an intake of approximately 2410 kcal (1560 + 850)

Energy fuel

Like fuel for a car the energy we need has to be blended. The blend that we require is approximately as follows:

— 57% Carbohydrates (sugar, sweets, bread, cakes)

— 30% Fats (dairy products, oil)

— 13% Protein (eggs, milk, meat, poultry, fish)

The energy yield per gram of carbohydrate, fat and protein is as follows:

— Carbohydrate - 4 kcal

— Fat - 9 kcal

— Protein - 4 kcal.

So what does our 50-kg athlete require in terms of carbohydrates, fats and protein?

— Carbohydrates - 57% of 2410=1374 kcal - at 4 kcal per gram=1374 / 4=343 grams

— Fats - 30% of 2410=723 kcal - at 9 kcal per gram=723 / 9=80 grams

— Protein - 13% of 2410=313 kcal - at 4 kcal per gram=313 / 4=78 grams

Our 50kg athlete requires: 343 grams of Carbohydrates, 80 grams of Fat and 78 grams of Protein

The types of fat

The nature of the fat depends on the type of fatty acids, which make up the triglycerides. All fats contain both saturated and unsaturated fatty acids but are usually described as 'saturated' or 'unsaturated' according to the proportion of fatty acids present. As a rough guide saturated fats are generally solid at room temperature and tend to be animal fats. Unsaturated fats are liquid at room temperature and are usually vegetable fats - there are exceptions e.g. palm oil, a vegetable oil which contains a high percentage of saturated fatty acids.

— *Unsaturated* - Sunflower oil, Olive Oil, Rice Oil, Nuts, Rapeseed Oil, Oily fish - Sardines

— *Saturated* - Beef, Bacon, Cheese, Butter, Biscuits, Crisps

The types of carbohydrates

There are two types of carbohydrates - starchy (complex) carbohydrates and simple sugars. The simple sugars are found in confectionery, muesli bars, cakes, biscuits, cereals, puddings, soft drinks and juices, jam and honey but remember these foodstuffs also contain fat. Starchy carbohydrates are found in potatoes, rice, bread, whole grain cereals, semi skimmed milk, yoghurt, fruit, vegetables, beans and pulses. Both types effectively replace muscle glycogen. The starchy carbohydrates are the ones that have all the vitamins and minerals in them as well as protein. They are also low in fat as long as you do not slap on loads of butter and fatty sauces. The starchy foods are much more bulky so there can be a problem in actually eating that amount of food so supplementing with simple sugar alternatives is necessary.

Your digestive system converts the carbohydrates in food into glucose, a form of sugar carried in the blood and transported to cells for energy. The glucose, in turn, is broken down into carbon dioxide and water. Any glucose not used by the cells is converted into glycogen - another form of carbohydrate that is stored in the muscles and liver. However, the body's glycogen capacity is limited to about 350 grams; once this maximum has been reached, any excess glucose is quickly converted into fat. Base your main meal with the bulk on the your plate filled with carbohydrates and small amounts of protein such as meat, poultry and fish.

Carbohydrates for Performance

Following training and competition an athlete's glycogen stores are depleted. In order to replenish them the athlete needs to consider the speed at which carbohydrate is converted into blood glucose and transported to the muscles. The rapid replenishment of glycogen stores is important for the track athlete who has a number of races in a meeting. The rise in blood glucose levels is indicated by a food's Glycaemic Index (GI) and the faster and higher the blood glucose rises the higher the GI. Studies have shown that consuming high GI carbohydrate (approximately 1grm per kg body) within 2 hours after exercise speeds up the replenishment of glycogen stores and therefore speeds up recovery time. There are times when it is beneficial to consume lower GI carbohydrates, which are absorbed slowly over a longer period of time (2-4 hours before exercise). Eating 5-6 meals or snacks a day will help maximise glycogen stores and energy levels, minimise fat storage and stabilise blood glucose and insulin levels.

Eating and Competition

What you eat on a day-to-day basis is extremely important for training. Your diet will affect how fast and how well you progress and how soon you reach competitive standard. Once you are ready to compete, you will have a new concern, your competition diet. Is it important? What should you eat before your competition? When is the best time to eat? How much should you eat? Should you be eating during the event? And what can you eat between heats or matches? A lot of research has been done in this area, and it is clear that certain dietary approaches can enhance competition performance. A future Successful Coaching Newsletter will address these issues.

Food composition tables

Food composition tables are widely used to assess nutrient and energy intakes, and to plan meals. The composition of food can vary widely, depending, among other factors, on the variety of plant or animal, on growing and feeding conditions and, for some foods, on freshness. Tables are based on average values from a number of samples analysed in the laboratory and therefore only provide a rough guide.

Nutritional Tips

Skipping meals or reducing your calorie intake does not help control weight in the long term. It is important to eat at regular intervals, ideally every 3-5 hours, as this helps to keep blood sugar levels stable.

Most of us do not drink enough water. Symptoms of dehydration include dizziness, lack of concentration, irritability and headaches. Aim to drink 6-8 glasses of water a day and you will stay well hydrated.

Your mother was exactly right when she forced you to eat up your greens. We should be eating 5 servings of fruit and vegetables a day for general health. To allow your vegetables to retain as much goodness as possible, put them into a pot of boiling water and cook them quickly.

Beware the hidden fat foods, which are normally those tasty party foods quiche, sausages, pork pie, salami, and dips are some examples. Of course biscuits, cakes and desserts should also be kept to a minimum and only eaten as a special treat. When you buy yoghurt go for low 'live bio' versions. These help to restore the 'good' bacteria that aid digestion.

Bread, potatoes and pasta are all carbohydrate foods that have received bad press in the past. These foods do not make you fat on their own. However, if you have a big cheese sandwich, knob of butter on your potato, or make a rich cream sauce for the pasta you will increase the amount of fat you are eating.

Alcohol taken in moderation can be beneficial to health, but if you are watching your weight it is relevant to know that the calories from alcohol cannot be used as fuel for exercise, nor do they provide any vitamins, minerals or fibre.

The butter versus margarine debate continues to rage. The best advice is not to eat a lot of either, but to eat a little of both. The best oil for cooking is Extra Virgin Olive Oil. It is not the cheapest but a little goes a long way.

Dairy products are a high source of fat and cholesterol, but they do provide us with other beneficial nutrients. The best approach is to buy "low fat" versions of milk, cheese, yogurt etc. as they will provide you with all the nutrients without the fat element.

It is not necessary to cut meat out of your diet. Instead buy the leaner cuts and trim off any fat. It is also recommended to eat oily fish (tuna, mackerel, herrings) at least 3 times a week as they contain the beneficial Omega 3 oil.

Achieving a balanced diet for vegetarian athletes

Many people, athletes and non-athletes, restrict or avoid meat or other animal products for religious, cultural or health-related reasons. The recommendation of a diet rich in carbohydrate may lead many athletes to one form of a vegetarian diet. There are many ways to be a vegetarian. A strict vegetarian, known as a vegan, eats no animal products at all. Lactovegetarians add milk and other dairy products such as cheese to their all-vegetable diet. Ovo-lactoyegetarians eat both eggs and milk products. A new group, which could be called semi- vegetarian, avoid red meat, such as beef and pork, but eat fish and poultry in addition to their ovo-lactoyegetarian diet. Additionally, emphasis is placed on foods that are "organic" and unprocessed and unrefined.

The major concern about vegetarian diets has always been the question of obtaining a balanced intake of nutrients. While a lactovegetarian and ovo-vegetarian diet may cover all nutritional needs, there may be a shortage of iron, calcium, iodine, selenium, zinc, riboflavin, vitamin D and vitamin B12 in a strictly vegetarian diet. Iron intake may also be low in a lactovegetarian diet because of the lack of haem iron from meat sources, which is more absorbable and improves the absorption of iron from vegetable sources. In addition, a higher dietary content of vitamin C is very useful to enhance iron absorption. Large amounts of tea and coffee may reduce the iron availability. Foods like green vegetables, some legumes and cereals have a relatively high content of non-haem iron.

Food combining for proteins

To receive a balanced distribution of essential amino acids, the vegetarian must eat vegetables that possess "mutual supplementation" of dietary protein. This is a nutritional strategy in which vegetable foods with low contents of amino acids (cereals, for example) are eaten together with a food that is high in that same amino acid (for example, milk and beans). In order to obtain an intake of good-quality proteins in the diet, the following food combinations are recommended:

— pasta with cheese
— rice and milk pudding
— cereals with milk or egg
— potatoes with egg or cheese
— rice and beans
— lentils and bread

If care is taken to include a wide variety of foods and to combine the right foods, vegetarian diets, except the strict or "pure" vegetarian way of eating, can be nutritionally adequate, and will not harm one's performance.

Do not be misled by the books

In many popular books say that the fail to recognise that our bodies can digest both protein and carbohydrates at the same time. By separating the two nutrient categories, as the diets in these books recommend, you will fail to achieve the benefits of mutual supplementation of dietary protein e.g. the vegetable protein (from bread) and the animal protein (from cheese). In general, the practical advice given in these books fails to meet recommended servings of calcium rich dairy products and energy rich complex carbohydrates from bread, cereals and potatoes. Remember that the greater the variety of foods we eat, the more we reduce the likelihood that we will develop a deficiency of any single nutrient.

In short, if athletes are to become vegetarians, they simply need a little more knowledge and must put more thought and planning into their diet. It may also be advisable to monitor iron status and blood profile in order to prevent iron deficiency anaemia. Female athletes should eat enough milk products, which are the best sources of calcium, in order to prevent osteoporosis. A well-balanced diet containing all food groups with the majority of vegetables, fruits and cereals in combination with the right amount of animal food is the sound base of nutrition for fitness and sport.

How to ensure your athletes eat healthily

Food provides the nutrients to help the body function properly. No single food contains them all in the amounts needed so a mixture of foods has to be eaten. Food is broken down into food groups of which there are five commonly accepted ones:

1. Bread, cereals and potatoes
2. Fruit and vegetables
3. Milk and diary foods
4. Meat, fish and alternatives
5. Fatty and sugary foods.

To get the wide range of nutrients the body needs to remain healthy it is important to choose a variety of foods from the first four groups every day. Foods in the fifth group (fatty and sugary foods) are not essential to a healthy diet but add extra choice and taste.

Bread, other cereals and potatoes

Includes	Other cereals means things like breakfast cereals, pasta, rice, oats, noodles, maize, millet and cornmeal. Beans and pulses can be eaten as part of this group.
Nutrients	Carbohydrate (starch), Fibre, some calcium and iron, B Vitamins
How much	Eat lots
Try to eat	Wholemeal, wholegrain, brown or high fibre versions where possible
Try to avoid	Having them fried too often (e.g. chips) Adding too much fat (e.g. thickly spread butter, or margarine on bread) Adding rich sauces and dressings (e.g. cream or cheese sauce on pasta)

Fruit & Vegetables

Includes	Fresh, frozen and canned fruit and vegetables and dried fruit. A glass of fruit juice can also contribute. Beans and pulses can be eaten as part of this group.
Nutrients	Vitamin C, Carotenes, Folates, Fibre and some carbohydrate
How much	Eat lots.
Try to eat	A wide variety of fruit and vegetables.
Try to avoid	Adding fat or rich sauces to vegetables (e.g. carrots glazed with butter, roast parsnips)Adding sugar or syrupy dressing to fruit (e.g. stewed apple with sugar)

Milk & dairy foods

Includes	Milk, cheese, yoghurt and fromage frais. This

	group does not include butter, eggs and cream.
Nutrients	Calcium Protein, Vitamin B12, Vitamins A and D
How much	Moderate amounts and choose lower fat versions whenever you can.
Try to eat	Lower fat versions means semi-skimmed or skimmed milk, low fat (0.1% fat) yoghurts or fromage frais, and lower fat cheeses (e.g. Edam, Half-fat Cheddar, Camembert).Check the amount of fat by looking at the nutrient information on the labels. Compare similar products and choose the lowest - for example 8% fat fromage frais may be labelled low fat but is not actually the lowest available.

Meat, fish and alternatives

Includes	Meat, poultry, fish, eggs, nuts, beans and pulses. Meat includes bacon and salami and meat products such as sausages, beef burgers and pate. These are all relatively high fat choices. Beans, such as canned baked beans and pulses are in this group.Fish includes frozen and canned fish such as sardines and tuna, fish fingers and fish cakes.
Nutrients	Iron, Protein, B Vitamins - specially B12, Zinc and Magnesium
How much	Eat moderate amounts and choose lower fat versions whenever you can.
Try to eat	Lower fat versions means things like meat with the fat cut off, poultry without the skin and fish without batter. Cook these foods without added fat. Beans and pulses are good alternatives to meat as they are naturally very low in fat.

Fatty and sugary foods

Includes	Margarine, low fat spread, butter, other spreading fats, cooking oils, oily salad dressings or mayonnaise, cream, chocolate,

	crisps, biscuits, pastries, cake, puddings, ice-cream, rich sauces and fatty gravies, sweets and sugar.
Nutrients	Some vitamins and essential fatty acids but also a lot of fat, sugar and salt
How much	Eat fatty and sugary foods sparingly - that is, infrequently and/or in small amounts.
Try to eat	Some foods from this group will be eaten every day, but should be kept to small amounts, for example; margarine, low fat spread, butter, other spreading fats, cooking oils, oily salad dressings or mayonnaise. Other foods from this group really are occasional foods, for example; cream, chocolate, crisps, biscuits, pastries, cake, puddings, ice-cream, rich sauces and fatty gravies, sweets and sugar.

How much do we need

People differ in the amount of calories they require each day and that is what affects the amount of food, in total, that individuals should eat. However much people need, the proportions of food from the different groups should remain the same. The factors that affect people's daily energy requirements are:

— *Gender* - women tend to need less calories than men

— *Age* - older adults need less calories than adolescents and young adults

— *Overweight* - being heavier than their ideal weight means less calories is required to achieve a healthy weight

— *Physically active* - the more active a person is, the greater their calorie needs

Vitamin and mineral supplements

Vitamin and mineral supplements cannot replace good eating habits. Most people can get all the nutrients their body needs by choosing a variety of foods, in the proportions shown, from the five food groups.

Some people may need certain supplements. Women who are already, or planning to become pregnant need folic acid, and, may need extra iron. Elderly people may need extra Vitamin D and/or iron. People should consult a doctor or dietitian if they think they need to take a vitamin or mineral supplement.

Food and Body Weight can Develop Eating Disorders

If you are an athlete aiming to optimise performance in your sport, you can obviously reap benefits from paying attention to what you eat. However, for some people this interest develops into an unhealthy obsession with food, calories and body weight. They worry continuously about what they are going to eat, when and where they are going to eat, how much weight they will put on if they go out for a meal with friends, how many hours they will have to exercise to burn off those calories, how they can avoid eating "banned" foods, and so on. Such an obsession with food and body weight is termed an eating disorder.

Eating disorders appear to be on the increase in the population as a whole. The number of people seeking treatment for anorexia and bulimia in one London hospital has increased by 360% over nine years. Experts have argued that one factor is a fashion ideal of the perfect body which has become progressively thinner over the last 40 years. Such media based pressure used to apply predominantly to women, but in recent years use of the male "body beautiful" in advertising has increased, leading to growing concern among men about whether their body conforms to the ideal.

Increased awareness and diagnosis may have also made an impact on the statistics. Research has identified a number of other factors thought to contribute to the development of eating disorders. Studies of twins indicate that genetic factors may play a part. Biological factors such as imbalances in neurotransmitters in the brain may be involved. Various psychological factors have also been proposed.

Here, the eating disorder is seen as a reaction to one or more of the following: being brought up in a family which has difficulty in resolving conflict and expressing emotions, actual or feared sexual abuse, difficulty in coping with stress, low self esteem. Overly simplistic diagnoses of causes should be avoided, however, as individuals will vary with respect to the primary causes.

Increased risk of eating disorders for athletes

Studies have shown that athletes are far more prone to developing eating disorders than non athletes. In addition to all the factors outlined above, athletes face additional pressures related to performance and, for some, aesthetic demands. For some athletes, such as distance runners, sprinters and swimmers, low body weight is thought to confer a competitive advantage. On the other hand, competitors in sports where a subjective judging element is involved, such as gymnastics, diving, skating and dancing may feel that their body size will influence their score. And certain sports where weight categories are involved, such as wrestling and rowing, can lead to cycles of weight gain followed by sudden weight loss.

Athletes often have heightened body awareness, making them more prone to body image concerns. Finally, perfectionism, compulsiveness and high achievement expectations are personality traits thought to be advantageous for the competitive athlete; however these very traits are commonly associated with the development of an eating disorder.

Thus, as might be expected, the highest prevalence of eating disorders is in female athletes competing in sports where leanness and/or a specific weight are considered important for either performance or appearance. Males also suffer from eating disorders, but at a lesser rate. The estimated proportion is one male for every 10 females.

Anorexia, bulimia and sub clinical disorders

The eating disorders, anorexia nervosa and bulimia nervosa, are recognised as types of psychiatric illness, and are clinically defined by a set of diagnostic criteria. These go beyond a concern with weight and body image, and also include serious psychological problems. A number of studies have identified a significant proportion of athletes who suffer from one of these disorders. Others, however, will exhibit less severe, or "sub clinical", forms of eating disorders that meet some but not all of the diagnostic criteria. Some experts have proposed that eating disorders are best conceptualised as a spectrum e.g. Fries has proposed a continuum hypothesis of eating/dieting behaviour which suggests that dieting may lead to disordered eating behaviours, which in turn may lead to anorexia nervosa or bulimia.

The concept of sub-clinical anorexia was first examined by researchers in the 1970s. It was later identified in adolescents exhibiting a pattern of growth failure and/or delayed puberty, due to self imposed calorie restriction arising from a fear of becoming obese.

Using case study information, another researcher adapted the concept of sub-clinical anorexia to athletes. The "sub-clinical anorexic" was described as a young male athlete strongly committed to his sport, who underwent extreme weight loss as a means of improving his chances of success. Eventually, the dieting and maintenance of an unrealistically low body fat were no longer the means to an end (i.e. athletic success), but became the end in itself. More recently, a Norwegian nutritionist has proposed a set of distinguishing features of a form of sub clinical anorexia she refers to as "anorexia athletica".

Attempts to define anorexia athletica

Sundgot-Borgen defines anorexia athletica in terms of absolute criteria (which must be present) and relative criteria (may be present). These are:

— Criteria that must be met:
 — Weight loss, gastrointestinal complaints, absence of medical illness or affective disorder explaining the weight reduction, excessive fear of becoming obese, restriction of calorie intake.

— One or more of the following:
 — Delayed puberty, menstrual dysfunction, disturbance in body image, use of purging methods, binge eating and compulsive exercising.

Researchers from Arizona State University have claimed that these criteria are somewhat ill defined and indiscriminate. They suggest that more research is needed to further delineate and define the unique characteristics of those with sub clinical eating disorders such as anorexia athletica. They make their own suggested list of absolute and relative diagnostic criteria, with the caveat that the number of criteria needing to be met remains to be determined. Their list is summarised as follows:

Absolute criteria

— Preoccupation with food, calories and body shape
— Distorted body image

— Intense fear of gaining weight or becoming fat even though moderately or extremely underweight

— Over at least a one year period, the athlete maintains a body weight below "normal" (5 to 15%) for age and height, using one or a combination of the following:

  — restricting energy intake

  — severely limiting food choices or food groups

  — excessive exercise (i.e. more than necessary for success in sport or as compared to athletes of similar fitness levels)

— Absence of medical illness or affective disorder explaining the weight loss or maintenance of low bodyweight

Relative criteria

— Gastrointestinal complaints

— Menstrual dysfunction

— Frequent use of purging methods (self induced vomiting, or use of laxatives or diuretics for at least one month)

— Bingeing (at least eight episodes a month for at least 3 months)

Causes

There has been considerable speculation about why athletes are at such increased risk for eating disorders (clinical and sub-clinical). It is hard to pin down which comes first. Is it a predisposing personality or life circumstances which lead both to athletic participation and an eating disorder, or does participation in certain sports cause the onset of the eating disorder? It seems likely that there will be some interaction.

A comprehensive study of elite female athletes undertaken in Norway sought to identify risk factors for eating disorders, along with trigger factors responsible for precipitating their onset or exacerbation. An initial screening questionnaire was sent to all elite female athletes in Norway. The 522 athletes responding represented six groups of sports: technical, endurance, aesthetic, weight dependent, ball games, and power sports.

The Eating Disorder Inventory was used to classify individuals at risk for eating disorders. 117 (22.4%) athletes were thereby defined as at risk, and 103 of these agreed to being given a clinical interview to diagnose eating disorders. A comparison group was also interviewed, consisting of 30 athletes chosen at random from a pool not at risk. These control subjects were matched to the at risk subjects for age, community of residence, and sport.

Ninety two of the at-risk athletes met criteria for anorexia nervosa, bulimia nervosa, or anorexia athletica. All of these athletes were asked if they had any suggestions as to why they had developed an eating disorder. 85% of these gave reasons. Information collected during the interviews was then combined with the specific reasons given by the athletes to define possible trigger factors associated with the development of eating disorders.

The results showed that athletes competing in the aesthetic and endurance sports were leaner and had a significantly higher training volume than athletes competing in the other sports. The prevalence of eating disorders was significantly higher among athletes in aesthetic and weight dependent sports than in the other sport groups.

Risk factors for eating disorders in athletes

Several risk factors were identified. Dieting at an early age appeared to be associated with the onset of an eating disorder. A significant number of athletes who began dieting to improve performance reported that their coach recommended they lose weight. For young and impressionable athletes, such a recommendation may be perceived as a requirement for improved performance. Other researchers have reported a similar syndrome e.g. finding that 75% of female gymnasts who were told by coaches that they were too heavy used unhealthy weight control measures.

The results of the Norwegian study also suggested that the risk for eating disorders is increased if dieting is unsupervised. Athletes with eating disorders may not seek supervision for fear their disorder will be discovered. In addition, many athletes have little knowledge about proper weight loss methods and receive their information in haphazard ways, from friends, magazine crash diets, and so on. Such diets are unlikely to account for the high energy requirements resulting from training, or the fact that maturing females have special nutritional requirements. Unsuitable crash diets may appeal to athletes if they feel that rapid weight loss is necessary to make the team or to remain competitive. Finally, the restrictive diets and fluctuations in body weight that accompany these efforts may also increase risk for eating disorders.

Early start of sport specific training was also associated with disordered eating. A higher percentage of athletic controls than of eating disorder athletes participated in other sports before choosing their preferred sport. An individual's natural body type usually steers the athlete to specific sports, and body type dictates in part whether the athlete will be successful. Beginning training for a specific sport before the body matures might have hindered these athletes from choosing a suitable sport for their adult body type. This could provoke a conflict in which the athlete struggles to prevent or counter the natural physical changes precipitated by growth and maturity.

Extreme exercise in itself has previously been cited as a potential causal factor in anorexia nervosa. In the Norwegian study, many of the athletes who did not give specific reasons for the onset of their eating disorder reported a large increase in training volume and a significant weight loss associated with the increased activity.

Athletes who increase their training volume may experience relative calorie deprivation, possibly because of not realising that they need to eat more to meet the increased energy demand, or perhaps due to reduced appetite produced by changes in endorphins. This calorie deprivation may create a biological or psychological climate in which eating disorders are more likely to develop. It has been observed previously that starvation itself can bring about symptoms of eating disorders e.g., obsession with food and hyperactivity.

Finally, the loss of a coach occurred in some athletes with eating disorders. These athletes described their coaches as vital to their athletic careers. Other athletes reported that they developed eating disorders at the time of injury or illness, which left them unable to train at high levels. Thus, the loss of a coach, injury, or illness must be seen as traumatic events that become trigger events for the onset of eating disorders.

Diagnostic criteria for bulimia nervosa

— Re-current episodes of binge eating. An episode of binge eating is characterised by both of the following:

- — Eating in a discrete period (e.g., within any two hour period) an amount of food that is definitely larger than most people would eat during a similar period of time and under similar circumstances
- — A sense of lack of control over eating during the episode (e.g. a feeling that one can not stop eating or control how much one is eating)

— Recurrent, inappropriate compensatory behaviour to prevent weight gain such as: self-induced vomiting, misuse of laxatives, diuretics or other medications, fasting, or excessive exercise

— The binge eating and inappropriate compensatory behaviours both occur, on average, at least twice a week for 3 months

— Self evaluation is unduly influenced by body shape and weight

— The disturbance does not occur exclusively during episodes of anorexia nervosa

Subtypes

— Purging type

- — The person regularly engages in self induced vomiting or the misuse of laxatives or diuretics

— Non purging types

- — The person uses other inappropriate compensatory behaviours, such as fasting or excessive exercise, but does not regularly engage in self induced vomiting or the misuse of laxatives or diuretics

Diagnostic criteria for anorexia nervosa

— Refusal to maintain body weight at or above a minimally normal weight for age and height e.g.

weight loss leading to maintenance of body weight less than 85% of that expected, or failure to make expected weight gain during a period of growth, leading to body weight less than 85% of that expected

— Intense fear of gaining weight or becoming fat even when under weight

— Disturbance in the way one's body weight or shape is perceived, undue influence of body weight or shape on self evaluation or denial of the seriousness of the current low body weight

— In females who have been menstruation the absence of at least three consecutive menstrual cycles

Subtypes

— Restricting types

 — Do not regularly engage in binge eating or purging behaviour (self induced vomiting or the misuse of laxatives or diuretics)

— Binge eating and purging types

 — Regularly engage in binge eating or purging behaviour

Prevention

Prevention is the key to addressing the problem of disordered eating, and education is a necessary first step. Athletes, parents, coaches, athletic administrators, training staff and doctors need to be educated about the risks and warning signals of disordered eating. Mimi Johnson, in "Disordered Eating in Active and Athletic Women" identifies the following checklist of warning signs:

1. A preoccupation with food, calories and weight
2. Repeated expressed concerns about being or feeling fat, even when weight is average, or below average

3. Increasing criticism of one's body
4. Secretly eating, or stealing food
5. Eating large meals, then disappearing, or making trips to the bathroom
6. Consumption of large amounts of food not consistent with the athlete's weight
7. Bloodshot eyes, especially after trips to the bathroom
8. Swollen parotid glands at the angle of the jaw, giving a chipmunk like appearance
9. Vomiting, or odour of vomiting in the bathroom
10. Wide fluctuations in weight over short periods
11. Periods of severe calorie restriction
12. Excessive laxative use
13. Compulsive, excessive exercise that is not part of the athlete's training regimen
14. Unwillingness to eat in front of others (e.g., team mates on road trips)
15. Expression of self deprecating thoughts following eating
16. Wearing layered or baggy clothing
17. Mood swings
18. Appearing preoccupied with the eating behaviour of others
19. Continuous drinking of diet soda or water

If you are concerned that someone you know may be suffering from an eating disorder, you need to go softly in approaching them about it. People who are truly anorexic or bulimic will often deny the problem, insisting that there is nothing wrong. Share your concerns about physical symptoms such as light headedness, chronic fatigue or lack of concentration. These health changes are more likely to be stepping stones for accepting help. Do not discuss weight or eating habits directly. Avoid mentioning starving/bingeing as the issue, and focus on life concerns. Offer a list of sources of professional help. Although the athlete may deny the problem to your face, they may secretly be desperate for help.

Seven Reasons why a low Carbohydrate Diet is wrong

Obesity is reaching epidemic levels in America and is now the second leading cause of preventable deaths. The medical community used to see it as simply the result of poor eating habits or a lack of will power but now they are beginning to define obesity as a disease that poses a dire threat to our public health. Low carbohydrate diets have become popular as the solution in our battle to lose weight. Unfortunately the human body is equipped to use carbohydrate as its primary source of fuel. Sadly the latest low carbohydrate fad diets are not the fuel the human body was designed to run on. Low carbohydrate diets can cause several health concerns over time. Here are my top seven.

1. Poor exercise performance and recovery

Carbohydrates are the primary fuel for your muscles and brain. Eating a low carbohydrate diet prevents proper maintenance of muscle and liver glycogen, decreasing muscle performance and increasing muscle fatigue. ATP is the main source of energy for all muscle contraction. When a muscle is used, a chemical reaction breaks down ATP to produce energy. There is only enough ATP stored in the muscle for a few contractions. More ATP is needed. There are three enzyme systems that can create more ATP.

The three sources of ATP for muscle contraction are carbohydrates, fatty acids and amino acid proteins. Carbohydrates metabolise efficiently and are therefore used first. If carbohydrates are not available, your muscles metabolise fatty acids and amino acids as secondary sources of ATP. These secondary sources are not efficient, which consequently cause your strength and endurance to drop drastically. It needs to be customised to your amount of muscle and exercise schedule. It provides 50% of your calories from high fibre, low glycaemia carbohydrates which are metabolised into muscle energy best. This will lead to increases in strength and muscle endurance.

2. Gout

Gout is a form of arthritis that occurs when excessive uric acid levels, start to crystallise in joints, leading to pain and inflammation. Uric acid is a waste product in the liver's metabolism of protein. Excessive amounts of protein may lead to an inability of elimination of uric acid.

3. Kidney stones

Kidney stones are hard masses that form in the kidneys when uric acid or calcium oxalate crystallises and over time form stones. Insoluble fibre found only in carbohydrates reduces the absorption of calcium, which cause urinary calcium levels to drop resulting in prevention of kidney stone's formation.

4. Constipation and poor intestinal health

To maintain good intestinal health our bodies require thirty or more grams of fibre daily. Fibre is divided into two types soluble and insoluble. Insoluble fibre is vital in formation of stools and decreases the time process of waste elimination. Low carbohydrate diets are too low in insoluble fibre and increase risk of constipation. Poor transit time of waste material increases risk of certain colon cancers. Insoluble fibres prevent the build up of mucus on intestinal walls which lead to poor absorption of nutrients into the body. Low carbohydrate diets are inadequate to maintain good intestinal wall health. This lowers the risk for constipation, irritable bowel, diverticulitis, crohn's disease, haemorrhoids and colon cancers.

5. Rise in cholesterol levels and an increased risk of heart disease

The risk of heart disease increases on low carbohydrate, low fibre diets. These diets promote excessive amounts of animal protein, cholesterol and saturated fat. Exuberant amounts of protein increase homocysteine, which is a bi product of the amino acid methionine. Many experts believe that high homocysteine levels have many toxic effects which lead to increase risk of heart disease and hardening of arteries. Low carbohydrate, low fibre diets reduce the absorption and elimination of digestive bile in the intestines. Digestive bile is produced in the liver from cholesterol. A decrease in digestive bile production raises blood serum cholesterol levels which increases the risk of heart disease. Unlike low carbohydrate diets would promote a nutritional balance providing 30% protein, 50% high fibre carbohydrates and 20% fat.

6. Osteoporosis

Osteoporosis is the reduction of bone density, due to the loss of calcium over long periods of time. Several dietary factors increase the risk of osteoporosis. When dietary protein reaches excessive levels, so does the loss of calcium in the urine. Most studies show that a life - long high protein diet results in an increase of osteoporosis. Poor intestinal health due to low fibre diets cause inadequate absorption of calcium in intestines contributing to poor bone formation.

This would suggest that all low carbohydrate diets cannot become a life long lifestyle of eating. This is only one of many reasons why low carbohydrate diets provide poor Long Term Weight Control. Interestingly, a diet too low in protein can also increase risk of osteoporosis. There is no one size fits all when managing our weight so it has to be customised to the individual providing the right balance of protein, carbohydrate and fat.

7. Loss of muscle and reduction of metabolism

Any diet that applies the restriction of calories less than the body's daily requirements over long periods of time will result in the loss of lean muscle tissue and a decrease in the metabolism. All low carbohydrate diets are focused solely on weight loss. The loss of fat comes at a high cost, which is the loss of lean muscle.

The loss of muscle reduces the resting metabolic rate, which is the major cause for rebound weight gain. Research shows 95% of all dieters' will regain that weight back. We do not fail at diets - diets fail us! The secret is not to try to lose fat every day as this will result in losing muscle and reducing metabolism.

ATP Production

Though energy is needed for all cellular function, the focus of this article is muscle contraction and body composition. All muscle contraction derives energy from adenosine triphosphate or ATP. The primary source of ATP comes from glucose, which is stored in the muscles and liver as glycogen (glucose and water). Muscle contraction during anaerobic activity (resistance training) can use glycogen directly to form ATP. The process is anaerobic glycolysis, meaning it can use the glucose as energy with very little oxygen (90% glucose, 5% oxygen and 5% fatty acid). Our muscles only store enough ATP for short periods of muscle contraction, when depleted leads to muscle failure. The rest period between weight training sets allows additional ATP to be produced. During early stages of aerobic exercise, ATP is again created primarily from glucose until the heart and lungs provide enough oxygen to the muscles to allow fatty acids to be used to create ATP. So there you have it during resistance training and the beginning stages of aerobic training the primary source of fuel is glucose. This supports my claim that low carbohydrate diets and exercise make poor partners. To uncover why, we need to quickly look at the concept behind low carbohydrate diets and how they work.

Low carbohydrate diets

Any diet that provides 100 grams or less of carbohydrate daily will quickly deplete the glycogen stores in the muscle and liver. This by itself is testimony that our muscle's primary source of fuel is glucose. Fatty acids stored in the adipose tissue (fat cells) are now released into the blood and processed by the liver and some are turned into glucose (gluconegenesis) and some remain fatty acids and both provide ATP for muscle contraction. One of the by products of this process is ketone bodies which can provide energy to brain and nervous system. The problem gluconegenesis (non glucose turned into glucose) provides fuel to the muscle less efficiently than glycogenesis (glucose). The end result is increased muscle fatigue, decreased muscle power, which leads to poor athletic performance.

Low Carbohydrate study

A recent study performed at the University of Connecticut showed that exercisers who switched from a balanced diet (proteins, carbohydrates and fats) to a low carbohydrate diet experience the following drops in athletic performance. There was a 7 to 9% drop in muscle power and 6% drop in VO2 max of cardiovascular performance. Another factor to consider is the recuperation of muscle between workouts is decreased on low carbohydrate diets.

So why would someone go on a low carbohydrate diet, especially when exercising?

Because the initial weight loss that comes from the glycogen depletion is believed to be fat loss. We have become so focused on weight loss, that any weight loss is seen as good. As identified earlier in this article glycogen is a mixture of glucose and water and the majority are stored where? You guessed it, the muscle. A large percentage of the initial weight loss is coming from muscle loss. The goal of exercise should be to improve body composition, the percentage or ratio of muscle to body fat. This can only be accomplished by losing fat without the loss of muscle tissue. Maintaining muscle mass is vital to sustainable weight control. The following steps will protect your muscles as your losing fat, while reaching your ideal weight and ideal body composition.

1. Cycle fat burning days with recovery days

The secret to losing fat without losing muscle starts with not being too aggressive or extreme with your reduction of carbohydrates. You need carbohydrate management, not carbohydrate elimination. Over the last 12 years, with more than 10,000 clients have found by reducing carbohydrates by 20% of daily needs and within 48 hours replenishing the glycogen in the muscle by eating 100% of daily carbohydrate requirements, allows for fat loss, without muscle loss. In essence you have two fat burning days, then a recovery day. By doing this you will have the best of both worlds. You will experience fat loss that averages between 1 to 2 pounds weekly, while muscles are being well fed. You never drastically deplete the glycogen stores in the muscle so athletic performance is not affected like on a low carbohydrate diet.

2. Exercise on days where you are receiving more carbohydrates

Exercising on days where muscles are getting more carbohydrates for fuel and taking days off from exercise when you are being aggressive about fat loss. One of the most difficult thoughts for exercisers to accept is that most of the results from exercise come when we are not exercising. They come after we exercise and in direct response to how the muscles receive nutrition after exercise.

3. Exercise 1½ to 2 hours after eating when blood sugar levels and insulin levels are slowly declining

As insulin levels increase in response to a rise in blood sugar after a meal, the cells are in an anabolic state. Insulin is the hormone that feeds are cells. As blood sugar levels drop, insulin levels drop and the pancreas produces the hormone glycogen and nutrients stored in the fat cells are released to the blood and used for energy. The management of this blood sugar rise and drop is important. If blood sugar levels go to high insulin feeds the muscle cells and deposits excess into fat cells. If insulin levels go too low, the muscle cells are being under fed. A slow rise in blood sugar provides good nutrition to the muscles and a slow drop allows glycogen to take from the fat cells. Timing your exercise to this blood sugar decline allows the muscles to receive from the fat cells more effectively. It is important to never exercise without having at least one meal left in your day so that muscles can recuperate from exercise.

Training and protein needs

You have decided to start bodybuilding but all of these new terms seem to be in a different language. Most of us experienced bodybuilders have felt the same way at one time, so do not give up just yet. You train hard, but you do not know anything about proper nutrition. Getting enough protein is most important when trying to develop a good body shape.

Why eat protein?

When consumed, protein turns into amino acids which become the cornerstone of muscle gain. Protein also helps you achieve muscle gain while keeping fat to a minimum. You need to space out your meals five to seven times a day to keep your metabolism at its best. Eating more meals also keeps your body in an anabolic state. To keep from getting board with your diet, your meals should never be from the same protein source at back-to-back meals.

Types of protein

Lean proteins that are low in fat should be eaten through out the day. Good protein sources to eat throughout day include egg whites, chicken breasts, tuna, and lean steak. There are many other good sources of lean protein but those examples will give you an idea of what to eat. Post workout is the best time to consume whey protein because your body absorbs it at a much faster rate than any other type of protein. Post workout is the only time of the day you should consume whey because your body absorbs it to fast to keep you adequately energised throughout the day.

Effects of a lack of protein

The obesity epidemic would be lower if people simply started eating more protein. It does not matter if you weight train or not, not getting enough will cause many health problems. A loss of muscle tissue is the main problem but do not expect to lose any fat either. Instead, fat gain will occur because of increased cortisol levels that are associated with lack of protein. Your immune system will start deteriorating, all of your body's cells will become weak and you will be more susceptible to illness.

Word of warning

Protein intake significantly above the recommended values can prove harmful because excessive protein breakdown strains the liver and kidney functions through the production and elimination of urea and other solutes.

How to recognise the early signs of eating disorder

Prevention is the key to addressing the problem of disordered eating, and education is a necessary first step. Athletes, parents, coaches, athletic administrators, training staff and doctors need to be educated about the risks and warning signals of disordered eating.

Warning signs

Mimi Johnson, in "Disordered Eating in Active and Athletic Women" identifies the following checklist of warning signs:

— A preoccupation with food, calories and weight
— Repeated expressed concerns about being or feeling fat, even when weight is average, or below average
— Increasing criticism of one's body
— Secretly eating, or stealing food
— Eating large meals, then disappearing, or making trips to the bathroom
— Consumption of large amounts of food not consistent with the athlete's weight
— Bloodshot eyes, especially after trips to the bathroom
— Swollen parotid glands at the angle of the jaw, giving a chipmunk like appearance

— Vomiting, or odour of vomiting in the bathroom
— Wide fluctuations in weight over short periods
— Periods of severe calorie restriction
— Excessive laxative use
— Compulsive, excessive exercise that is not part of the athlete's training regimen
— Unwillingness to eat in front of others (e.g., team mates on road trips)
— Expression of self deprecating thoughts following eating
— Wearing layered or baggy clothing
— Mood swings
— Appearing preoccupied with the eating behaviour of others
— Continuous drinking of diet soda or water.

If you are concerned that someone you know may be suffering from an eating disorder, you need to go softly in approaching them about it. People who are truly anorexic or bulimic will often deny the problem, insisting that there is nothing wrong. Share your concerns about physical symptoms such as light headedness, chronic fatigue or lack of concentration. These health changes are more likely to be stepping stones for accepting help. Do not discuss weight or eating habits directly. Avoid mentioning starving/bingeing as the issue, and focus on life concerns. Although the athlete may deny the problem to your face, they may secretly be desperate for help.

Drink your way to Winning Performances: the Seven Secrets of Hydration

If you wish to perform at a high level, you need to consume fluid. For each per cent of body weight lost due to dehydration, your performance slips by about 2%, and a meagre 2% loss in weight can force your heart rate and body temperature to spiral upward, making strenuous exercise almost impossible to carry out.

If you are going to be exercising for 20 minutes or less, dehydration is not usually a problem, but difficulties can arise during longer exertions. For example, copiously sweating athletes can flush about 1.5 litres of fluid per hour through their sweat glands, a total of three pounds per hour. If these heavily perspiring individuals weight 150 pounds that is a 2% loss in weight after just one hour producing a 4% dip in performance if no fluid is taken on board. The downturn in performance would be smaller, about 2%, after 30 minutes, but that is still enough to make a difference to serious athletes who are interested in winning.

But what are the rules for fluid intake? How much do you really need and what should your drink be like? To make it easy for you, we have listed the seven rules of fluid intake during exercise below. If you follow these rules, you will keep your body water intact during exercise and perform at a much higher level.

Rule 1: The rate of passage of water from your stomach into your small intestine depends on how much fluid is actually in your stomach. If there is lots of water there, fluid flow from stomach to intestine is like a springtime flood; if there is little water, the movement resembles a lightly dripping tap. Therefore, to increase stomach intestinal flow you need to deposit a fair amount of liquid in your stomach just before you begin your exercise. Intake, 10 to 12 ounces of fluid is a good start. This will feel uncomfortable at first, so practice funneling this amount of beverage into your "tank" several times before an actual competition.

Rule 2: To sustain a rapid movement of fluid into your small intestine during your exertions, take three to four sips of beverage every 10 minutes if possible, or five to six swallows every 15 minutes.

Rule 3: If you are going to be exercising for less than 60 minutes, do not worry about including carbohydrate in your drink; plain water is fine. For more prolonged efforts, however, you will want the carbohydrate.

Rule 4: Years of research have suggested that the correct concentration of carbohydrate in your drink is about 5 to 7%. Most commercial sports drinks fall within this range, and you can make your own 6% drink by mixing five tablespoons of table sugar with each litre of water that you use. A bit of sodium boosts absorption; one third teaspoon of salt per litre of water is about right. Although 5 to 7% carbohydrate solutions seem to work best for most individuals, there is evidence that some endurance athletes can fare better with higher concentrations. In research carried out at Liverpool John Moores University cyclists who ingested a 15% maltodextrin solution improved their endurance by 30% compared to individuals who used a 5% glucose drink. The 15% drink also drained from the stomach as quickly as the 5% one, though many other studies have linked such concentrated drinks with a slowdown in water movement.

Rule 5: A 6% "simple sugar" drink will empty from your stomach at about the same rate as a fancy, 6% "glucose polymer" beverage, so do not fall for the idea that the latter can boost water absorption or enhance your performance more than the former, and do not pay more for the glucose-polymer concoction.

Rule 6: Contrary to what you have heard, cold drinks are not absorbed into your body more quickly than warm ones. However, cold drinks are often more palatable than warm ones during exercise, so if coldness helps you to drink large quantities of fluid while you exert yourself, then keep your drinks cool.

Rule 7: Swilling drinks during exercise does NOT increase your risk of digestive system problems. In actuality, most gut disorders that arise during exercise are caused by dehydration, not from taking in fluid. Dehydration induces nausea and discomfort by reducing blood flow to the digestive system, so by all means keep drinking!

Are you getting enough fluids?

An adult human is made up of 55 to 65% water, which is equivalent to about 9 gallons (40 litres) and is vital to sustain life and is a key ingredient in all body cells and fluids. We can last a lot longer without food (up to 80 days) than water (3 to14 days). Part of the reason for this is that we can store substantial energy reserves as fat, which has a high ratio of energy to its volume, but water cannot be compressed. Unfortunately, fat is not easy to convert to energy for the sort of levels of "fuel" consumption required by an athlete. This is why we use carbohydrate-based diets.

For any sort of power output we need to transport "fuel" (glycogen) from its "tank" (liver) to the "engine" (muscles). Fluid is the most efficient way of transporting this "potential power". In the case of a car it is the oil that lets the bearings run smoothly, for us it is blood. If you think of oil in a car, it becomes less efficient as it gets old, petrol gets used up and needs replenishing and you need water in your radiator to stop the engine overheating and seizing. In all these cases the key to the best and most efficient performance is to keep the fluids fresh and topped up!

So how much do we need and what grade should it be?

Like cars, humans are not all the same. Look at us! We get everything from clapped-out bangers, which would not pass an mot, to high-performance dragsters that go like rockets, but would struggle with a 3-point turn. In between there are family cars, off-roaders, container trucks, motorcycles and a mass of others; but all have one thing in common - they need the right fluids to run and we are the same. So, effectively water is a catalyst that lets us work properly:

— It transports nutrients such as glycogen, salts and oxygen to the right parts of the body
— It removes waste products such as lactic acid from muscles through the bloodstream and from the kidneys in the form of urine
— It helps regulate our body temperature between strict limits in the form of sweat
— It lubricates the joints and eyes
— It assists breathing
— It maintains blood pressure and volume

On this basis, it is vital we maintain our levels of fluid when stressing the "engine" (body) in sport.

How much water do we use in a day?

It depends who we are, what we are doing and where. An average, an inactive individual of 75kg (about 12stone) in a mild climate will use about 2½ litres of water a day (see table below); that is half-a-gallon.

Daily water input		*Daily water losses*	
Food	1000ml	Urine	1250ml
Drinks	1200ml	Faeces	100ml
Metabolism	350ml	Skin	850ml
		Lungs	350ml
Total	2550ml	Total	2550ml

How much do we need to be drinking?

The answer is to always make sure it is enough. Fluid loss is a great short-term way of appearing to lose weight, but it is only temporary and can have serious effects on athletic performance. Just 2% loss will affect your performance and a 5% loss could lead to as much as 30% loss of power output. That may sound like quite a lot. For our 75kg individual, it would mean nearly 4 kilos of water, but if they were 2% below optimum to start, then the loss of just over 2kg will have them hitting the 95% barrier. On a hot day on a bike this can happen very quickly due to sweat loss.

The thought of having to drink half-a-gallon of water each day while you are at rest may seem a bit daunting - it is. This figure includes the water content of foods, which can be quite substantial. For instance, on a "per edible portion" basis (i.e. not per 100g), tomatoes can have a water content of 93g and white fish 82g, while crisps have just 2g. However dried dates, which are a good energy source, have 12g water but potatoes have 79g water per portion. The solution is perhaps to take an interest in what you eat and drink. When you exercise you will lose a lot of weight simply through the fluid losses. However, there is also a bit of weight lost by using up energy in the form of glycogen that is formed from fat, protein and carbohydrate intake.

But how much do we lose?

As an example, a 10-mile cycling time-trial will probably use about 500kcals, which constitutes about 65grams (2.3oz). If you lose more than that - you are dehydrating.

Regulation of body water balance

The following table is a recommended daily intake of water for a sedentary individual with body mass of 70 to

75kg living in temperate climate. (Intake = food + drinks + metabolism)

Age	Intake ml/kg body weight	(i.e. For 75kg individual)
12 years	58	4.35 litres
20 years	35	2.625 litres
50 years	35	2.625 litres
60 years	30	2.25 litres

Water content of food - per edible portion

Tomatoes	93g water
Melon	92g water
Milk	88g water
White fish	82g water
Potatoes	79g water
Low fat spread	50g water
Butter, margarine	16g water
Dried dates	12g water
Crisps	2g water

Why do we sweat?

Exercising muscles produce heat, but the body's temperature needs to keep within safe limits, around 37 to 38° C. In order to do this we work in a similar way to a car's engine, we use a radiator for water-cooling. Sweating is the major way of getting rid of heat from the body (by evaporation). Unlike a car's system, which is sealed and so re-circulates cooled water, ours allows the fluid to evaporate and so needs regular topping up to maintain performance.

Rate of sweating depends on several factors

— *Work rate* - If you indulge in more physical work,

you use more energy and create more heat, so need more cooling, which needs more sweat

— *Environmental temperature* - If it is warm, your body does not have to work so hard to maintain its temperature. If it is working hard, it will need more cooling than where the environments assisting in the cooling process already. Wind and wind-chill work in the same way. In this respect a cyclist that is putting out the same wattage as a runner will get colder because they are travelling faster and getting a greater airflow over their sweating body

— *Humidity* - The humidity or moisture content of the air affects how easily sweat can vaporise from the skin into the atmosphere. In high humidity, sweating will be less effective because it is harder to transfer to "wet" atmosphere than "dry". Think of trying to squeeze a sponge out underwater rather than over a bucket, which will remove its water faster? Alternatively, consider which environment a boxer or jockey uses to lose fluid weight quickly, a Turkish bath or a sauna?

— *Body surface area* - This is interesting and requires a little maths. You may think a big, fat individual has a greater surface area, so should be able to sweat more than a small person and cool off faster. Unfortunately, they also have a larger core to regulate the temperature of and because the core size increases at roughly 3 times the speed of the surface area, the surface area of a large individual will have to work much harder to keep them cool! On the other hand, the small person will be much more prone to hypothermia when they get cold.

— *Hydration status* - If you are dehydrated already, your body is going to do a balancing act between avoiding further, possibly dangerous, dehydration and (also possibly dangerous) overheating. One way of doing this would be to stimulate cramps so you do not use so much energy and do not need so much cooling. Whatever happens, it is unlikely to be conducive the maximum performance, so keep the balance right!

— *Training status* - A trained athlete (with adapted muscles, heart and lungs) will be able to perform more efficiently, effectively and therefore more economically than an untrained one. This means they will not need to sweat so much for a given level of effort because their "engine is" better tuned.

— *Clothing* - Wearing the right gear may sound obvious, but it is worth keeping up with materials technology. Gore-Tex has made a fantastic difference in volume and breathabilty of clothing. Wicking under-vests also make the journey more comfortable and can assist in the process of temperature regulation.

How dehydration can affect performance

It is really important to know how well hydrated you are as well as weight and body-fat percentages. This used to be quite expensive and complicated to find out but can now be done with scales that are widely available for less than £100. If that is still too expensive, it may be worth considering buying a set as a group (maybe a sports club). The only caveat would be to make sure they are cleaned properly between users to avoid risks of passing foot problems such as verrucas between users. The scales work by passing a small pulse between the feet and measuring the resistance, compared with the user's age, height and sex.

Accuracy is normally pretty good and permits a graphic record of improvements in weight, fat and hydration management.

— Dehydration by as little as 2% loss of body weight starts to impair performance

— Dehydration in excess of 5% loss of body weight can decrease work capacity by 30%

— Heat illness can occur when 5 to 6% body weight is loss

What actually happens?

— Muscular strength/power is affected

— Prolonged moderate to high intensity activity is most susceptible to dehydration due to the problem of getting the body to perform at high level AND take on more fluids to maintain hydration at the same time

— Perception of effort is increased for the same workload - you feel more fatigued or reduce your self-selected pace

— Effects occur at all levels of dehydration and increase as the degree of dehydration increases.

— Myth - "Dehydration can be tolerated" - it cannot, any dehydration will reduce performance.

— Dehydration reduces mental functioning:

  — Decision making
  — Reaction times
  — Concentration
  — Anticipation
  — Skill delivery
  — Task inaccuracies.

To sum up - monitor yourself

— Record your body weight before and after exercise and allow for different types of weather

— 1kg weight loss is equivalent to 1 litre of sweat lost
— Pee test - monitor colour, volume and frequency
— Keep a record of fluid intake
— Know your own requirements.

Fat Loss

Always make carbohydrate intake a priority

In the early stages of physical adaptation the body will have to, "learn" how to utilise fat as a priority fuel source. This takes some weeks to achieve with regular practice on cardiovascular exercise. This raises another crucial point. If there is not enough carbohydrate available each day then you will have to utilise some of your already low amount of lean tissue protein, and convert it to simple sugar (glucose) through the Glucose - Alanine chain in the liver.

So in order to try and burn some fat you have had to sacrifice some of your already low lean tissue protein stores to enable fat to be burnt in the mitochondria in the presence of carbohydrate & oxygen. This means that you are actually losing lean tissue and gaining a proportionate percentage of fat tissue. This is a scary fact which slows down any measurable difference in your lean / fat percentage ratio.

Always remember that fat loss is all about long term goals

Burning fat takes time, but the more you do it the easier it becomes and the greater the amount of fat burned will be. When performing fat burning exercise it takes about 20 minutes for an unconditioned person to actually start burning fat. An average conditioned person will take about 10 minutes, whereas an elite Tour De France athlete takes only about 5 minutes. This is an important fact as it shows that for an unconditioned person, 20 minutes of fat burning exercise is not enough. The aim, therefore, is to progressively and safely reach 45 minutes. It takes a fit person about 11 sessions of a 45 minutes fat burning exercise period to burn 1 lb of fat, which is 3500 kcal. People new to exercise will always take longer.

Never alternate between cardiovascular equipment when performing fat burning cardiovascular work

It is generally accepted that when you come off one piece of cardiovascular equipment and go onto another, that it is going to take between 8 to 10 minutes before you reach full fat burning potential again on the subsequent piece of cardiovascular equipment. However this will depend on your level of fitness and your percentage of Red Slow Twitch and Intermediate Twitch muscle fibres. The fitter you are and the more aerobic and intermediate muscle fibres you have, the quicker you will reach the fat burning zone again.

In addition to this, during any 4 to 6 or 8 to 12 week fat burning meso cycle you must always use exactly the same exercises during the entire meso cycle so that you ensure maximum muscle fibre recruitment and that the body can learn the most effective way in which to perform this exercise, the most efficient way of processing nutrients and removing waste products, and also the best way of maintaining and recovering from the demands imposed. The stationary exercise bike without moving handles is the best piece of equipment for performing your fat burning cardiovascular work on, as it keeps the heart rate at a much more stable level. This means that you can get the maximum amount of fat burning possible out of each session by keeping your heart rate in the correct zone throughout the entire session.

As the day progresses, the metabolic rate falls. So in the late evening and early hours of the morning, your body is at its most inefficient for processing large quantities of fuel in one go. However, this does not mean that you cannot eat after 6 pm, of course you can. In fact, it is essential that you do eat again to make sure that your metabolic rate is kept as high as possible. The only thing that you have to bear in mind is that you must keep this food intake to a snack, whilst making sure that it is of good nutritional value. If you eat nothing from the early evening onwards, your body is essentially in starvation mode until you wake and eat breakfast the next morning. This has two very important implications.

The first is that your body thinks that starvation is really a possibility, as it has no way of knowing that you are trying to lose body fat. As a result the body dramatically lowers the metabolic rate in order to counter the possibility of starvation and thus conserve as much energy as possible. Secondly, a significant amount of carbohydrate depletion occurs whilst you sleep. By not eating anything at all from the early evening onwards you will also have completely decimated your carbohydrate stores by the time that you wake again, which will ultimately have a negative impact upon your long term training goals.

Never eat too little

It is generally accepted that 1 or 2 pounds is the very maximum amount of fat that you can lose in a week without sacrificing intra-cellular water and lean muscle tissue. In order to achieve this, the maximum calories you can cut from your diet is 1/7 which equals about 15% of the total calorie intake. This limited reduction will also ensure that you lose body fat without slowing down your metabolic rate.

Never choose low in fat, always choose low in calorie

Low in fat does not equate to low in calorie. A lot of these products are filled with sugar in order to make them taste better. Always check the calorie content to make sure that you are in fact buying something that is low in calorie.

You are going to have to face the fact that if you want to lose body fat then you are going to have to put in a little effort. Convenience foods are high in chemicals, salt, and a host of other harmful substances. In addition, the majority of convenience foods offer little nutritional value. Everyone will use these from time to time, but the more you can do without the better it will be.

8

Training Plan for Swimmers

The sport of swimming demands athletes and coaches who are very meticulous in their preparation for competition. In no other sport is the level of preparation, tapering for the big day and rigid control of training intensities quite the same. One aspect that contributes to this accuracy in training pace is the uniformity of conditions. Apart from having a warmer or colder pool or one that is 25, 33.3 or 50m in length, there is little difference in the training environment. Let us face it, you are all staring at a black line on the pool floor for length after length.

Demands of the Sport

There can be variety within the sport, however, depending quite simply on which stroke(s) are your best and you use in competition, as well as on what distance you travel on race day. This means that there is an element of specialisation in swimming, much as Linford Christie and Rob de Castella have somewhat diverse approaches to running.

A 25 metre swim would give a similar competition time to the 100m sprinter, while a 200 metre effort could give a race duration between 1:30 to 2 minutes, and an endurance event of 1500m may require between 14 to 20 minutes, depending on age, standard and gender.

. This range of events means that a variety of forms of conditioning are needed to match the demands of the race event. Although a training regimen of mixed paces will be used by all swimmers, the sprinter will clearly be logging fewer but faster training lengths for preparation, while the endurance counterpart will log considerably more lengths at a more sedate tempo.

Which events you are best at will he governed more by genetics than training. It is unrealistic for an athlete whose muscles are composed predominantly of slow twitch fibres to have dreams of Olympic gold at the shorter events, but the experienced coach will soon direct aspiring youngsters to the correct race distance.

Phases of Training

Planning the perfect peak, to coincide with the most important gala on the yearly calendar, is the hallmark of the world class swimmer and coach. The training year will typically start from the active rest enjoyed at the end of your previous season. The planning of various training phases, however, will work back from competition day of the following season. The key variables to play with are volume and intensity, while the influence of land work, especially strength training, will also sculpt your swimming fitness for a crescendo on the important race day. This could be anything from the Olympic Games to a national championships, county championships or local gala or club event. You must choose when your own big goal performance is to be.

It may be that you plan two peaks, one for the short-course season in winter and another for the long course. This double periodisation could mean that you have two general endurance periods, two specific endurance periods, the two competition periods, as well as two taper periods, all within a year. Naturally these periods will be much shorter than in a single periodised year. How you structure your training within these periods is a matter of preference, but there will probably be greater volume in the general endurance period, followed by a period of moderate to high volume with increased intensity. This is then followed by a period of taper, which leaves your body fresh and ready for competition, with lots of training banked up from which to draw.

The Training Week

A whole host of different types of training sessions can fit into the week of the swimmer, giving the coach and physiologist ample opportunity for workouts of slightly different intensity. The structure of the week will vary according to the particular phase but it is important that all aspects are covered to different degrees, all year round.

Four major intensities can be established and these in turn may well be sub-divided to give a greater range of options. In Base Endurance sessions, you work at very low intensities to enhance the oxidative capacity of the muscles and increase the ability to metabolise fats as an energy substrate. Aerobic maintenance sessions will form a large bulk of volume, where the intensity is a little harder to give a greater stimulus to the heart and lungs. Threshold work should give the optimal aerobic training effect, provided the intensity is right. If you are too fast, there is a greater contribution from anaerobic metabolism, and if you are too slow, you could be going faster. Speed endurance, or lactate production and lactate tolerance sessions are far more intense and so need to be done in interval workouts to keep sufficient volume.

Added to these conditioning sessions should be flexibility work, before and after pool sessions, and in sessions in their own right. Technique work is also vital in a sport where hundredths of a second really count. Work in the weight room can increase strength and power, a crucial factor in swimming success, but it is important to choose exercises that are actually going to contribute to an increase in swimming velocity. If they are not specific to your sport, then the value of time spent on such work is, at best, questionable.

An exercise routine is correctly planned and properly adhered to, then improvements in physical strength will result as the body adapts to the load. Exercise is one method of making the body accustom itself to handle the imposed training loads. For adaptation to take place, the following must be given strict attention to during both the planning stages and the implementation of the plan afterwards.

— The stimulus magnitude, more commonly referred to as overload

— Accommodation

— Specificity

— Individualisation

The Stimulus Magnitude

The correct amount of stimulus or overload brings about positive changes in the athlete's physical state. This load must be greater than what the body is normally accustomed to for a positive change to take place. There are two ways to manage the adaptation process. One is to increase the intensity or volume, and the second is to select different exercises.

Training loads are divided into the following categories:

— *Stimulating* - the magnitude of the load is above the neutral level which allows positive physical changes to take place

— *Retaining* - also known as the neutral zone as the body is just maintaining its present condition
— *Detraining* - too much of a good thing causes a deterioration in performance, the functional capabilities in the athlete or both the performance and functional abilities

Accommodation to Training

Accommodation to training is the second part of the adaptation process. If the same load and the same set of exercises are consistently used time after time the body soon adapts, and then stops making progress.

"This is a manifestation of the biological law of accommodation, often considered a general law of biology". According to this law, the response of a biological object to a given constant stimulus decreases over time. Thus, accommodation is the decrease in response of your body to a constant continued stimulus. In training, the stimulus is physical exercise."

Inefficiency occurs due to the accommodation law if standard exercises and training loads are used over long periods. Training stimulus must vary in order to be beneficial.

This training stimulus must be as specific as possible to the sport or activity one is training for in both muscular coordination and physiological demands. A high transfer of training results when using specific exercises during the training session.

However, these two requirements (the same standard exercises and training loads) present problems for the elite athlete. The training has to be variable to avoid accommodation and yet stable enough to satisfy the demands of specificity.

To avoid the staleness that accompanies accommodation, qualitative and quantitative alterations are made to the plan. Quantitative changes are those changes made to the training loads. Qualitative differentiation results in the selection of different yet specific exercises. Elite athletes require broad qualitative changes to their programs to remain on top of their sport.

Specificity of Training

Specificity of training is the holy grail of all sports coaches. Without specificity, the sessions are a waste of effort and time. Almost every coach and athlete knows that resistance training increases muscle mass and strength, and that endurance training provides positive changes in aerobic capabilities.

Described another way, specificity simply means a transfer of training effect to the sport or activity being trained for in the first place. But why is this transfer so important? Because of the positive results on the playing field, that's why.

Standard deviations of measurement indicate the crossover effect of properly designed specificity training regimens to be dependent upon movement velocity, joint angle, and production of force amongst others. These must mimic the actual sport conditions in the areas previously mentioned.

Individualisation of Training

Everyone is different and the same training program will not work for everyone. It is ludicrous to set up a professional, college or experienced athletes' routine for a novice strength athlete. Yet it is done in countless High Schools worldwide every single day.

If the coaches would take the underlying principles of the program and make the necessary modifications to fit their athletes then positive adaptive progressions would be the result. These principles should be creatively applied, not blindly applied straight across the board, but correctly applied.

Average routines are for average people and not for those with training experience. These individuals need special treatment in their program design. Routines are best made with the end result constantly kept at the forefront. With the athletes needs kept in the forefront and the two meshed together so the sum is greater than either part. Synergy of action, transference of training, hard work and fun all combine to produce a positive training effect on the athlete.

The FITT Principle ...in Relation to Injury Prevention

The FITT Principle (or formula) is a great way of monitoring your exercise program. The acronym FITT outlines the key components of an effective exercise program, and the initials F, I, T, T, stand for:

— F = Frequency which refers to how often you exercise

— I = Intensity which refers to how hard you exercise

— T = Time which refers to how long you exercise for

— T = Type which refers to the kind of exercise you undertake

What is the Mainstream Recommendation?

The FITT Principle is most commonly used in the weight loss industry, although it is also used as part of strength and weight training recommendations. The standard recommendation is as follows.

— Frequency - 5 to 6 times per week

— Intensity - Moderate to high

— Time - Anywhere from 15 to 40 minutes

— Type - Just about any exercise

The Components

Frequency

Frequency is a key component of the FITT Principle. Remember that it is important to know why you are exercising and what you wish to achieve before rushing into any exercise program. Adjust the number of times you exercise per week to reflect your current fitness level, the time you realistically have available, your other commitments like family and work, and the goals you have set for yourself.

Intensity

This is an extremely important aspect of the FITT principle and is probably the hardest factor to monitor. The best way to gauge the intensity of your exercise is to monitor your heart rate.

There are a couple of ways to monitor your heart rate but the best way by far is to purchase an exercise heart rate monitor. These can be purchased at most good sports stores and retail from $50 to $400. They consist of an elastic belt with a transmitter that fits around your chest and a wrist watch that displays your exercise heart rate in beats per minute (bpm).

If you do not want to spend the money on a heart rate monitor, simply count your heart rate over a 15 second period. All you need is a wrist watch that has a "seconds" display. Feel for your heart beat by either placing your hand over your heart or by feeling for your pulse in your neck or on your wrist. Count the beats over a 15 second period and then multiply by 4. This will give you your exercise heart rate in beats per minute.

Time

The time you spend exercising is also an important part of the FITT Principle. The time dedicated to exercise usually depends on the type of exercise undertaken. It is recommended that to improve cardiovascular fitness you will need at least 20 to 30 minutes of non stop exercise. For weight loss at least 40 minutes of moderate weight bearing exercise is required. However, when talking about the time required for muscular strength improvements, time is often measured as a number of "sets" and "reps." A typical recommendation would be 3 sets of 8 repetitions.

Type

Like time, the type of exercise you choose will have a big effect on the results you achieve. That is why it is important to know what you want to gain from your efforts. If you are looking to improve your cardiovascular fitness, then exercises like walking, jogging, swimming, bike riding, stair climbing, aerobics and rowing are very effective.

For weight loss any exercise using a majority of your large muscle groups will be effective. To improve muscular strength the best exercises include the use of free weights, machine weights and body weight exercises like push-ups, chin-ups and dips.

How does all this relate to Injury Prevention?

The two biggest mistakes, people make when designing an exercise program, is firstly training too hard, and secondly, not including enough variety.

The most common problem is that people tend to find an exercise they like and very rarely do anything other than that exercise. This can result in long term, repetitive strain to the same muscle groups, and neglect, or weakening of other muscle groups. Leading to a very unbalanced muscular system, which is a sure-fire recipe for injury.

FITT Principles

Frequency After you finish exercising your body goes through a process of rebuilding and repair. It is during this process that the benefits of your exercise are forthcoming. If you are exercising on a daily basis (5 to 6 times a week) then your body never has a decent chance to realise the benefits and gains from the exercise. What usually happens is that you end up getting tired or injured and just quit. My frequency recommendation is - only exercise 3 to 4 times a week maximum!

This may sound strange and a little hard to do at first, but after a while exercising like this becomes very enjoyable and something that you can look forward to. It dramatically reduces your likelihood of injury because you are giving your body more time to repair and heal. Many elite level athletes have seen big improvements in performance when forced to take an extended break. Most never realise they are training too hard, too often.

Intensity, Time and Type

The key here is variety. Do not let yourself get stuck in an exercise rut. In regards to intensity and time, vary your effort. Dedicate some of your workouts to long, easy sessions like long walks or light repetitive weights. While other sessions can be made up of short, high intensity exercises like stair climbing or interval training. Remember, if you are not feeling 100% then take the day off or schedule an easy workout. The type of exercise you do is also very important. Many people get into a routine of doing the same exercise over and over again. If you really want to lower your risk of injury then do a variety of different exercises. This will help to improve all your major muscle groups and will make you a more versatile all round athlete. Cross training is a great way of adding variety to your workout schedule.

Long and Winding Road to Marathon Improvement

The marathon: running it, coaching athletes to complete it and most of all coaching club runners who want to improve their performance. We are not talking about Olympians here, but of athletes who aim to break a personal goal of, say, 3.30, 3.15 or even 4.00 hours, often whilst balancing the needs of a job and a family. Many such athletes are offered a deluge of advice on the subject of training for improved marathon performance, all of it well meant, but much of it at best misguided. No wonder then that so often they become confused, disheartened, injured or disappointed. Hence this paper on my own practical steps for those coaching "mortal" athletes, seeking to perform at a higher level. It may not see them on the airplane to the next Olympics but it will provide them with good memories that last a lifetime.

Step One - Treat Each Athlete as an Individual

When discussing training with any athlete, bear in mind that a training program is unique for each athlete and that an approach of "one size fits all" is not the solution. Spend plenty of time understanding each athlete as an individual. Go through each training diary for the last year, and see the world from the athlete's eyes. What was the plan? Why was it like that? What went well? Talk about lifestyle. What time is really available to train? What gets in the way of training? What new opportunities for training time are there? What was the performance last time? What happened last time out (exactly, before, after and during, mile by mile)? What is the new performance goal? Why is that the goal? Piece together the evidence and reflect upon it before reaching conclusions. What factors strongly influenced the athlete's performance during the last attempt at the distance? How could they be overcome this time?

Step Two - Select a Goal Race Some Distance Hence

Fundamental to success is allowing plenty of time for preparation, especially where weekly mileage will become significantly increased. Twenty to thirty weeks of steady preparation may not be unreasonable, even from a good base level of fitness. Consider the environment - choose an event that will be fundamentally flat, and is likely to be cool. Choose an event that will attract a small field.

Step Three - Establish the Cornerstones of the Plan

Weekly Distance

As a "rule of thumb", 50 to 75 miles per week seems to hold a lot of merit. Anything less than 50 miles may not allow for V02 max improvement and more than 70 miles may bring diminishing returns and maybe career/ marriage threatening! Allowing plenty of build up time (increase distance by a maximum of 10% per week) is vital and check the training diary each week to ensure that no "extra" sessions are creeping in!

The long Run

In my view, extending the long run to the target race time (not distance), and repeating it at that level several times during preparation is key. Remember to schedule in plenty of recovery time between these sessions. Think again about the long run. How can you help your athlete to hold his or her pace steady at around one minute below goal pace? This is not just going to happen - you have to make it happen. Consider mile marking some favoured routes, or recruiting the stalwart pacers of your club as "sparring partners" to help your athlete to keep it consistent.

Speed training - is it appropriate?

Here is where even the real experts can disagree. Yet again let us remain practical; there has to be a planned level of running faster than goal pace, and a planned level of running exactly at goal pace. How else is goal pace going to become maintainable over the marathon? Think again about speed. Exactly how fast will your athlete need to run to achieve the goal? Does he or she even know? How exactly does that pace relate to half marathon pace, 10k pace, 800m pace and 400m pace? Consider a weekly track session, a weekly race-pace session and how you will progress these sessions as the weeks roll past. Do your own research on these subjects and start off by looking at Frank Horwill's superb on-line materials.

Recovery and rest

It is time to plan that active recovery and rest, it is just as important as the running. We all know it. We have all probably ignored it at times. Do not let your athlete make the same mistake and make certain that the rest is taken. And almost finally, let us not forget the taper. Research it, agree it and do it. And finally, let us not forget the night before and the morning before the race. In fact, let us plan it and rehearse it a dozen times in training. This should include the food, the drink, the kit, and the sleep. Find what delivers optimum confidence and performance for each individual and stick with it.

Step Four - Motivate

The sad fact is that for most mortals, training for a significant marathon performance improvement is not going to be great fun. Most often it will include extended periods of running in the dark and or rain, extended periods of grumbling from any loved ones on the scene, and extended periods of wondering if it would not be easier to focus on the 10k. What can you do to motivate and encourage your athlete? Can you create and help visualise a picture of success so compelling as to drive out those negative thoughts. Can you plan time to really listen to feedback and to inspire confidence? I hope that the above makes some practical sense.

In sports, as well as in life, it is very important to set goals for yourself. They provide direction so that you can achieve the things that will bring you happiness and success. When setting goals the succession of events goes like this: set a goal, have a detailed plan, commit to that plan, and then take action. Sound easy? It can be if you take goal setting seriously and approach it systematically.

Goals

First you need a long-term goal. A long-term goal is an objective statement about a specific achievement that can be measured. What is it the team ultimately wants to accomplish? Or, what is it I ultimately want to achieve? An example of this would be "to finish 50th or above at the end of season," or "to have a fielding percentage of at least 94% at the end of the season." When most players are asked what their goal is they typically reply, "I want to win," "Play in the pros," or "Be the best." These statements tell you little on how to achieve this and they do not direct your behaviour. It is very important for the team, coaches and individual players to have a long-term goal in mind. Approach your long-term goal incrementally - one game at a time, one practice at a time and one short-term goal at a time - otherwise it may seem too overwhelming and out of reach. Place all your efforts and energy into achieving this goal. Keeping in mind, "What is it I need to do to attain my definitive goal?" If you are not sure of numbers, a suggestion is to look at the numbers from last year, as well as the numbers of the team that won the league/conference and make a realistic assessment that way. Coaches should help their athletes set team goals, as well as encourage them to set individual goals that coincide with the team's goals.

One problem that teams tend to have is that they set long-term goals at the beginning of the season, then never go back to see how they are doing, and they do not really talk about their goals or strategies to get there. Former San Francisco 49er, Dr. Jamie Williams says, "Every team in the league will say they want to win the Super Bowl, but the 49ers take steps and strategies to achieve that goal, positive strategies. All things are pointed in the direction of that goal, which is why they are there." There must be consensus among the team in regards to the team goals, as well as an ongoing, periodic review and assessment of the goals so that they do not lose their effectiveness. Sometimes goals need to be adjusted along the way to keep them challenging, as well as realistic.

Then, it is important to set short-term and daily goals that lead up to the long-term goal. These become the stepping stones along the way. As you achieve each short-term goal your confidence will grow and you will be that much closer to the next one. Keep in mind, goal-setting plays an integral role in you achieving success, so it is important to take the time to set some goals!

Identifying goals

The importance of goal-setting, but you also need to be dedicated mentally and physically to achieving the goals you have set for yourself. Follow these practical tips to help you with that:

1. *Write down your goals:* This is a very important step! Clearly define what the results are that you desire. Once you know exactly where you're headed and what you expect to achieve, commit your objective to paper and verbalise it to someone. This reinforces

your sense of mission and devotion. Writing your goals down will help increase your dedication. Then, write down your progress in relation to the goals to use as feedback and motivation.

2. *Develop specific strategies:* Decide on the plan that will most efficiently accomplish your goals; i.e., the number of quality ground balls each practice, number of strikeouts for the next game, etc. Write it down and be specific. Remember, it is quality not quantity! The path you define must be very clear-cut and precise.
3. When devising your series of goals, use the divide and conquer rule. Divide monumental tasks into short-term goals. They will be more manageable and easier to reach; and, as you accomplish each one, you will enjoy positive reinforcement and a feeling of success.
4. Prioritise your goals; do not try to do too many things at once. Just assume responsibility for the goal you are working on at the moment - do not overwhelm yourself. Then, start working on an area where the slightest of improvement will be visible, this will help you stay committed to your goal setting.
5. Once you set your goal you need to sit down and plan out how you are going to achieve it, mentally and physically. First, you need to realistically assess where you are now and take into consideration what your current capabilities are. Then, decide what your long-term goal is. Halfway between the two becomes your mid-season goal. From there your mental and physical strategies/plans become your short-term goals that you work on a daily basis.
6. It is important that you keep your goals in line with things you have control over. You can control your

effort and the task you are working on; you can't control other people or the situation around you. Focus only on things within your control, this way you'll be less susceptible to distractions.

7. Keep a positive and healthy attitude about your sport. Remember, no one is perfect. We all have bad days, but do not let that destroy or hamper your motivation. Setbacks are inevitable. Always keep in mind your goals and objectives. If you do this every day, at the end of the season you will be able to be proud of what you've done, knowing that you did something each day to help you reach your goals.
8. *Give credit where credit is due:* Each day, congratulate yourself for completing the goal you set for that day. Enjoy the feeling of having taken another step towards your long-term goal.
9. *Own your goals:* For you to have the desire to take action you must own your goals and be committed to them. Your goals need to be your own, either set only by you, or in collaboration with your coach. You know best what you want and need to do. From there you need to internalise your goals so that they are a part of who you are, and where you want them to take you. Be passionate about your goals and be accountable for them. You must be consistent and follow through with your goal setting.
10. *Assess each new goal you make:* Am I willing to do what it takes to reach the goals I have set for myself? Do my daily/short-term goals go succinctly with my mid-season and long-term goals? How much control do I have over reaching my goals? Are there other ways of reaching my goals?

When setting your goals, keep these things in mind; and, do not forget . . . the journey of 1,000 miles begins with 1 step.

9

Planning for Success

An understanding of the training process is fundamental to planning, as is knowledge of the status of the athlete, their potential and indeed their goals. The matter is then developed to look at the latest literature affecting development of the key areas of speed, strength and skill (coordination). As one say that the development of performance in competition is achieved through a training process that is designed to induce automation of motor skills and enhance structural and metabolic functions.

Training also promotes self-confidence and a tolerance for higher training levels and competition...He continues '..sport activities are a combination of strength, speed and endurance executed in a coordinated and efficient manner with the development of sport-specific characteristics.' Stressing the relevance of planning: 'Short and long term planning (periodisation) requires alternating periods of training load with recovery.' A more recent publication extends the concept of periodisation and proposes new strategies for working with the concept while another looks specifically at planning for skill acquisition and the key factor of timing of competition readiness.

Planning Around Goals

Very often the planning stage is based around the needs of a particular competition phase or major event where the athlete needs to be at their peak. Classically, the approach here is to set this date down and work backwards from that point to the current date in order to identify the specific goals to be achieved along the way and to identify the appropriate timing of key elements of the plan. Effective planning is therefore based around the actual goal. Without a goal the planning cannot commence and a plan cannot be formulated. Two recent publications outline the key elements of goal setting for both coaches and athletes and the subsequent planning requirements. Well thought out planning will ensure the athlete has a positive experience and remains motivated along the road to ultimate goal achievement.

Monitoring and evaluation

Once a plan is implemented constant monitoring is critical in order to evaluate progress, in turn facilitating review and identifying any requirement for change. Once again, the planning stage will have identified key review times, their relevance and the options available at each stage. One recent note looks at the importance of monitoring training loads and proposes simple methods for monitoring. Clearly, a training plan with no objective or empirical means of monitoring loads cannot hope to achieve optimum results for an athlete. On a more specific point the need for performance evaluation along the way is also critical in providing feedback to the athlete, coach and other support staff. A note based on the evaluation of swimmers proposes that the first means of measurement should be competition itself followed by detailed technical analysis of that performance. Training 'efforts' and specific training sets where certain aspects are studied in depth would be the next level.

Then follows a host of physiological measurement options. Interestingly, especially following recent publications concerning strength and power development in swimmers, these factors appear fairly low down the list. The chapter continues with the supposition that the psychological skills and emotional competencies become more accentuated at higher performance levels and that the essence is, once again, in the planning and that only measurements appropriate to the athlete and their goals need be incorporated. Finally, the stresses the importance of correct interpretation of information and careful choice of action.

Dynamic progression

Along the same lines, but from a generic resistance training perspective, identifies the importance of strength, power, speed, hypertrophy, localised muscular endurance, motor performance, balance and coordination in improving athletic performance. The dynamic nature of progression is emphasized along with the importance of adapting the plan to achieve the goals.

Strength transferability

One question that has often puzzled coaches is the transferability of strength gains from limited to full range of lotion. A recent matter concludes that, based on a study of fifty women, assigned to one of four training groups for a specific quadriceps strength training regime over six weeks with a knee flexion range between 30 and 90 degrees, that the range of knee flexion used in each group during training had no bearing on the overall strength gain observed in isometric output at the end of the study as well as in the rate of force development both measured at 10, 45 and 80 degrees. As well as being useful for fully active athletes the potential benefit during rehabilitation is obvious.

Allowing for recovery

Muscle fatigue, a major limiting factor to performance, is a key consideration in session planning. He also relate this to slow twitch muscle fibres stating that their prevalence does not affect resistance to such fatigue or accelerate recovery from this form of training load. However, biopsy data is not reported and so this appears to be an assumption.

Aerobic conditioning for power athletes

Examination of the pattern of energy use during supra-VO2 maximal exercise and metabolic responses of both trained and active untrained subjects to repeated bouts of intense, constant power exercise, which was designed to deplete muscle glycogen, were evaluated. Sixteen males (trained and untrained) with similar genetic aerobic capacity were studied. Subjects ran repeatedly to exhaustion at 125% VO2max. Total exercise time was significantly greater in trained (42.75 ± 3.85 min) than untrained (33.10 ± 6.95 min) subjects. The trained subjects apparently spared glycogen during supra-VO2 maximal exercise presumably by oxidising more fat (in slow twitch fibres). Thus athletes who participate in anaerobic events may benefit substantially from aerobic training, as well as anaerobic training. Power athletes generally avoid endurance training but the benefits appear to be demonstrated with this chapter.

Speed for efficiency

Cyclists were the subject at pedaling cadence, efficiency and power output. The findings, based on a study of 8 professional cyclists, demonstrate that riding at high power output yields greater efficiency and economy at higher pedal cadences (100rpm) versus lower cadences (60rpm). The message seems to be to use a lower gear and higher cadence to maintain efficiency over 6 minute bursts.

Speed and speed endurance

Finding a correlation between a measurable gym based strength activity and speed sounds very useful and this is exactly what researchers looking at 17 elite football players have found. Maximal strength half squats correlated extremely well with 30m sprint times and vertical jump height. Unfortunately, no data is given to support the conclusion that improving half-squat performance actually improves sprinting speed. Staying on the subject of sprinting another say that identifies that fact that for maximal runs to exhaustion for 15 competitive male endurance athletes bicarbonate (82.3s), lactate (80.2s), citrate (78.2s) all produce an improvement over chloride when taken 90 minutes before runs. It would be interesting to see if the results altered in any way with variation in times of administration before runs since different digestive / biochemical pathways may be involved.

Specific flexibility and how to get it

The use of contract-relax Proprioceptive Neuromuscular Facilitation stretching (CRPNF) to enhance flexibility has been popular for some time. However, the scale of the voluntary contraction made by the athlete when performing CRPNF has not been studied. According to recent studies contractions as low as 20% of the maximal voluntary isometric contraction (MVIC) still yield the same benefits for enhancing hamstring flexibility based on a study of 72 male subjects. Furthermore, utilisation of lower MVIC's should reduce the risk of injury during CRPNF work. An interesting selection criterion was used for all participants - the inability to reach 70degrees of hip flexion during a straight leg raise - a very useful indicator for all coaches which may well correlate with propensity for hamstring injury in training / competition.

Flexibility and when not to do it

Many coaches commonly advocate static active stretching and two publications from the same group report the effect on force and jumping performance as well as force, balance, reaction time and movement. Conclusions were that an acute bout of stretching impaired the gains from the warm-up in terms of balance and movement time and, perhaps even more significantly improvements gained in the range of movement at this point led to a reduction in quadriceps torque or force by as much as 10.4% for up to 120 minutes after active stretching! The stretching debate has run around the world recently from a number of perspectives. This data, however, supports the previously held view of many coaches, but not hitherto taken seriously, since it was only viewed as 'anecdotal' evidence. It seems that major performance benefits can still be derived for many athletes through appropriate and optimal preparation on the day of competition. Finally, having done all the work and competed, how best to recover.

A cautionary message about massage

Sports massage is very popular and viewed as desirable by many sports. However, two recent resons fail to support the benefits expected from massage. One looks at limb and skin blood flow after concentric quadriceps exercise. The agreed desirable benefit would be to enhance femoral artery blood flow and muscle temperature. However, this did not occur even following deep effleurage and petrissage massage. Skin blood flow did increase but this may only serve to divert flow away from the recovering muscle thus questioning the efficacy of massage. The second thing was based on bilateral eccentric quadriceps exercise for 16 subjects and the measurement of loss of strength and recovery over a three-day period with and without massage. Massage treatment of one leg did not improve the level or duration of pain or recovery of strength when compared to the other untreated leg in all subjects.

Feeling better may be the key recovery parameter

A recent study of fifteen Japanese college rugby football players seems to point the way. Seven performed only normal daily activities and eight performed additional low intensity exercise during the post-match rest period. Players were examined just before, immediately after as well as one and two days after the match. Blood markers were used to assess physiological condition, and the profile of mood states (POMS) scores were examined to evaluate psychological condition.

Muscle damage recovered with time almost equally in both groups, but the POMS scores were significantly decreased only in subjects in the low intensity exercise group. Rugby matches impose both physiological and psychological stress on players. The addition of low intensity exercise to the rest period did not adversely affect physiological recovery and had a significantly beneficial effect on psychological recovery by enhancing relaxation.

This supports the belief that the body needs time to recover and then adapt to the training or competition load and that low level exercise or 'active' recovery in itself does not appear to facilitate this. However, psychological recovery is clearly of enormous importance when facing the next physical bout and will affect motivation to train or compete. Interestingly, neuromuscular recovery is thought to take significantly longer than physical muscular recovery - up to 5 times longer.

10

Performance Evaluation

Testing and measurement are the means of collecting information upon which subsequent performance evaluations and decisions are made. The whole measurement/evaluation process is a six stage, cyclic affair, involving:

— The selection of characteristics to be measured

— The selection of a suitable method of measuring

— The collection of that data

— The analysis of the collected data

— The making of decisions

— The implementation of those decisions.

All of the above stages should be completed with the athlete - especially the analysis and making decision of appropriate corrective action.

Requirements of a Test

In constructing tests it is important to make sure that they really measure the factors required to be tested, and are thus objective rather than subjective. In doing so all tests should therefore be specific (designed to assess an athlete's fitness for the activity in question), valid (test what they purpose to test), reliable (capable of consistent repetition) and objective (produce a consistent result irrespective of the tester).

In conducting tests the following points should be considered:

— Each test should measure one factor only
— The test should not require any technical competence on the part of the athlete
— Care should be taken to make sure that the athlete understands exactly what is required of him/her, what is being measured and why
— The test procedure should be strictly standardised in terms of administration, organisation and environmental conditions.

Benefits of Testing?

The results from tests can be used to:

— predict future performance
— indicate weaknesses
— measure improvement
— enable the coach to assess the success of his training program
— place the athlete in appropriate training group
— motivate the athlete.

Tests additionally break up, and add variety to, the training program. They can be used to satisfy the athlete's competitive urge out of season. Since they demand maximum effort of the athlete, they are useful at times as a training unit in their own right.

Influencing Factors for Test Results

The following factors may have an impact on the results of a test (test reliability):

- — The ambient temperature, noise level and humidity
- — The amount of sleep the athlete had prior to testing
- — The athlete's emotional state
- — Medication the athlete may be taking
- — The time of day
- — The athlete's caffeine intake
- — The time since the athlete's last meal
- — The test environment - surface (track, grass, road, gym)
- — The athlete's prior test knowledge/experience
- — Accuracy of measurements (times, distances etc.)
- — Is the athlete actually applying maximum effort in maximal tests
- — Inappropriate warm up
- — People present
- — The personality, knowledge and skill of the tester.

Why record information?

For the coach it is important to monitor the program of work, to maintain progression in terms of the volume of work and its intensity. Both coach and athlete must keep their own training records. A training diary can give an enormous amount of information about what has happened in the past and how training has gone in the past. When planning future training cycles, information of this kind is invaluable.

What should be recorded?

The information to be recorded falls into two broad categories: -

- — The day-to-day information from training
  - — State of the athlete (health, composure)

- — Physiological data (body weight, resting heart rate, etc.)
- — The training unit (speed, speed endurance, strength, technique)
- — The training load (the number of miles, the number of sets and repetitions, the number of attempts)
- — The training intensity (kilograms, percentage of maximum, percentage of VO2)
- — The prevailing conditions (wet, windy, hot etc.)
- — The response to training (the assignments completed, the resultant heart rate recovery, felt tired, etc.)

— Information that measures status. This can take the form of a test. If the test is repeated throughout the program, it can then be used as a measure of progress within the training discipline. Examples of such tests are:

- — Time trials - speed, speed endurance, endurance
- — Muscular endurance - chins, push ups, dips
- — Strength maximum - single repetitions, maximum repetitions
- — Explosive strength - power bounding, vertical jump, overhead shot putt
- — Mobility - objective measurements of the range of movement
- — Event specific

Competition evaluation

Following competition, it is important that the coach and athlete get together as soon as possible in order to evaluate the athlete's performance. Elements to be considered are pre race preparations, focus and performance plans and achievement of these plans.

Maximal Tests

Maximal means the athlete works at maximum effort or tested to exhaustion. Examples of maximal anaerobic tests are:

— 30m sprint

— Wingate 30 second cycle ergometer test

Examples of maximal aerobic tests are:

— Multistage Fitness Test

— Cooper Test

Disadvantages of maximal tests are:

— difficulty in ensuring the subject is exerting maximum effort

— possible dangers of over exertion and injury

— dependent on the athlete's level of arousal

Submaximal Tests

Submaximal means the athlete works below maximum effort. In sub maximal tests, extrapolation is used to estimate maximum capacity. Examples of submaximal aerobic test are:

— PWC 170 test

— Queen College step test

Disadvantages of submaximal tests are:

— depend on extrapolation being made to unknown maximum

— small measurement inaccuracies can result in large discrepancies as a result of the extrapolation

Normative data

Where normative data (average test results) is available, it is included on the appropriate evaluation test pages which are identified below.

Evaluation Tests

The following are examples of evaluation tests that can be performed with athletes:

Aerobic Endurance - VO2 max

2.4 Km Run Test

Testing and measurement are the means of collecting information upon which subsequent performance evaluations and decisions are made but in the analysis we need to bear in mind the factors that may influence the results.

Objective

The objective of this test is to monitor the development of the athlete's aerobic endurance.

Required Resources

To undertake this test you will require:

— 400 metre track

— Stop watch

— An assistant

How to conduct the test

— Athlete to complete a 10 minute warm up

— Athlete to complete the 2.4km (6 laps of a 400m track)

— Assistant to keep athlete informed of the number of laps remaining to complete the test

— Assistant to record the time taken for the athlete to run 2.4km

Analysis

Analysis of the result is by comparing it with the results of previous tests. It is expected that, with appropriate training between each test, the analysis would indicate an improvement.

Target group

This test is suitable for active athletes but not for individuals where the test would be contraindicated.

Reliability

Reliability would depend upon how strict the test is conducted and the individual's level of motivation to perform the test.

Astrand Treadmill Test

Testing and measurement are the means of collecting information upon which subsequent performance evaluations and decisions are made but in the analysis we need to bear in mind the factors that may influence the results.

Objective

To monitor the development of the athlete's general endurance (VO2 max).

Required Resources

To undertake this test you will require:

— Treadmill where the speed can be set at 5 mph (8.05 km/hr) and grade of slope can be adjusted

— Stopwatch
— An assistant.

How to conduct the test

The treadmill is set up at the start with a speed of 8.05km/hr (5 mph) and a grade of slope of 0%. The athlete commences the test. After 3 minutes, the grade is set to 2.5% (1.4°) and then every 2 minutes the grade is increased by 2.5% (1.4°).

The assistant starts the stopwatch at the start of the test and stops it when the athlete is unable to continue.

Analysis of the test result

Analysis of the result is by comparing it with the results of previous tests. It is expected that, with appropriate training between each test, the analysis would indicate an improvement.

From the total running time an estimate of the athlete's VO2max can be calculated as follows:

$$VO2\ max = (Time \times 1.444) + 14.99$$

"Time" is the total time of the test expressed in minutes and fractions of a minute.

The athlete stopped the test after 13 minutes 15 seconds of running (13.25 minutes).

— VO2 max=(13.25 × 1.444) + 14.99
— Vo2 max=34.123 mls/kg/min.

Target group

This test is suitable for endurance athletes and players of endurance sports (e.g. football, rugby) but not for individuals where the test would be contraindicated.

Reliability

Reliability would depend upon how strict the test is

conducted and the individual's level of motivation to perform the test.

BALKE VO2MAX TEST

Testing and measurement are the means of collecting information upon which subsequent performance evaluations and decisions are made but in the analysis we need to bear in mind the factors that may influence the results.

Objective

The objective of the Balke test is to monitor the development of the athlete's VO2 max.

Required Resources

To undertake this test you will require :

— 400m track

— Stop watch

— Assistant.

How to conduct the test

The Balke Test is conducted as follows:

— Choose a windless day and run around a track for 15 minutes

— The assistant notes the total distance run to the nearest 25 metres.

Analysis

Analysis of the result is by comparing it with the results of previous tests. It is expected that, with appropriate training between each test, the analysis would indicate an improvement.

Target group

This test is suitable for endurance athletes and players of endurance sports (e.g. football, rugby) but not for individuals where the test would be contraindicated.

Reliability

Reliability would depend upon how strict the test is conducted and the individual's level of motivation to perform the test.

Balke Treadmill Test

Testing and measurement are the means of collecting information upon which subsequent performance evaluations and decisions are made but in the analysis we need to bear in mind the factors that may influence the results.

Objective

To monitor the development of the athlete's general endurance (VO2 max).

Required resources

To undertake this test you will require:

— Treadmill where speed and grade of slope can be adjusted

— Stop watch

— Assistant.

How to conduct the test

The athlete walks on a treadmill to exhaustion. At timed stages during the test the grade of slope (%) of the treadmill is increased as follows:

— Active and sedentary men

- — Treadmill speed set at 3.3 mph
- — Start - Grade is 0%
- — After 1 minute - Grade set at 2%
- — After 2 minutes and each minute thereafter the grade is increased by 1%

— Active and sedentary women

- — Treadmill speed set at 3.0 mph
- — Start - Grade is 0%
- — After 3 minutes and every 3 minutes thereafter the grade is increased by 2.5% (1.4°).

The assistant starts the stopwatch at the start of the test and stops it when the athlete is unable to continue - this ideally should be between 9 and 15 minutes.

Analysis

Analysis of the result is by comparing it with the results of previous tests. It is expected that, with appropriate training between each test, the analysis would indicate an improvement.

From the total time an estimate of the athlete's VO2 max can be calculated as follows:

$$VO2\ max = 1.444 \times T + 14.99$$

"T" is the total time of the test expressed in minutes and fractions of a minute e.g. 13 minutes 15 seconds = 13.25 minutes.

From the total time an estimate of the athlete's VO2 max can be calculated as follows:

$$VO2\ max = 1.38 \times T + 5.22$$

"T" is the total time of the test expressed in minutes and fractions of a minute.

Target group

This test is suitable for active and sedentary individuals but not for those where the test would be contraindicated.

Reliability

Reliability would depend upon how strict the test is conducted and the individual's level of motivation to perform the test.

Cunningham and Faulkner Test

Testing and measurement are the means of collecting information upon which subsequent performance evaluations and decisions are made but in the analysis we need to bear in mind the factors that may influence the results.

Objective

The objective of this test is to monitor the development of the athlete's anaerobic capacity.

Required resources

To undertake this test you will require:

— Treadmill capable of 20% gradient

— Stop watch

— An assistant.

How to conduct the test

— The athlete undertakes a warm-up on the treadmill

— A few short practice starts getting onto the treadmill at the test speed should also be performed

— The treadmill is set at 8.0 miles/hr (12.9 km/hr) speed and incline of 20%

— The assistant starts the stopwatch when the athlete starts running unsupported
— The test continues until exhaustion, meaning the athlete cannot maintain the speed required
— The assistant records the time to the nearest 0.5 seconds.

Analysis

Analysis of the result is by comparing it with the results of previous tests. It is expected that, with appropriate training between each test, the analysis would indicate an improvement.

Target group

This test is suitable for active athletes but not for individuals where the test would be contraindicated.

Reliability

Reliability would depend upon how strict the test is conducted and the individual's level of motivation to perform the test.

RAST

Testing and measurement are the means of collecting information upon which subsequent performance evaluations and decisions are made but in the analysis we need to bear in mind the factors that may influence the results.

Objective

The Running-based Anaerobic Sprint Test (RAST) was developed at the University of Wolverhampton to test an athlete's anaerobic performance. RAST is similar to the Wingate ANaerobic 30 cycle Test (WANT) in that it provides coaches with measurements of power and fatigue index. The Wingate test is more specific for cyclists whereas the RAST provides a test that can be used with athletes where running forms the basis of the movement.

Required Resources

To undertake this test you will require:

— 400 metre track - with a 35 metre marked section on the straight
— Two cones to mark the 35 metre section
— Stop watch
— An assistant.

How to conduct the test

The athlete :

— is weighed prior to the test
— undertakes a 10 minute warm session
— has a 5 minute recovery
— completes six 35 metre runs at maximum pace (10 seconds allowed between each sprint for turnaround).

The assistant

— records the time taken for each 35 metre sprint to the nearest hundredth of a second
— makes appropriate calculations.

Analysis

Analysis of the result is by comparing it with the results of previous tests. It is expected that, with appropriate training between each test, the analysis would indicate an improvement.

Calculations

Power output for each sprint is found using the following equations

— Velocity = Distance ÷ Time

— Acceleration = Velocity ÷ Time

— Force = Weight × Acceleration

— Power = Force × Velocity

Or

— Power = Weight × $Distance^2 \div Time^3$

From the six times calculate the power for each run and then determine :

— Maximum power - the highest value

— Minimum power - the lowest value

— Average power - sum of all six values ÷ 6

— Fatigue Index - (Maximum power - Minimum power) ÷ Total time for the 6 sprints

Athlete weight = 76 Kilograms

Sprint	*Time (secs)*	*Power (watts)*
1	4.52	1008
2	4.75	869
3	4.92	782
4	5.21	658
5	5.46	572
6	5.62	525

Maximum Power = 1008 watts

Minimum Power = 525 watts

Average Power = 736 watts

Fatigue Index = 483 ÷ 30.48 = 15.8 watts/sec

505 Agility Test

Testing and measurement are the means of collecting information upon which subsequent performance evaluations and decisions are made but in the analysis we need to bear in mind the factors that may influence the results.

Objective

The objective of this test is to monitor the development of the athlete's speed and agility.

Required resources

To undertake this test you will require:

— 6 cones

— Non slip surface

— Stopwatch

— An assistant.

How to conduct the test

— Mark out the course as per the diagram above. The distance from A to B is 10 metres and the distance from B to C is 5 metres

— The athlete runs from the start line (A) towards the 10 metre line (B) (run in distance to build up speed)

— The assistant starts the stopwatch as the athlete passes through the 10 metre line (B).

— The athlete runs on to the 15 metre line (C), turns and runs back towards the start line

— The assistant stops the stopwatch when the athlete passes through the 10 metre line (B) on their return to the start line

— The best of two trails is recorded.

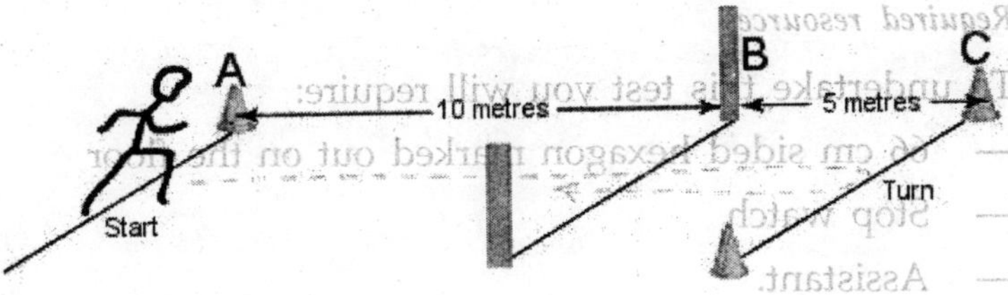

Analysis

Analysis of the result is by comparing it with the results of previous tests. It is expected that, with appropriate training between each test, the analysis would indicate an improvement.

Target group

This test is suitable for active athletes but not for individuals where the test would be contraindicated.

Reliability

Reliability would depend upon how strict the test is conducted and the individual's level of motivation to perform the test.

Hexagonal Obstacle Test

Testing and measurement are the means of collecting information upon which subsequent performance evaluations and decisions are made but in the analysis we need to bear in mind the factors that may influence the results.

Objective

The objective of the Hexagonal Obstacle test is to monitor the athlete's agility.

Required resources

To undertake this test you will require:

— 66 cm sided hexagon marked out on the floor

— Stop watch

— Assistant.

Illinois Agility Run Test

Testing and measurement are the means of collecting information upon which subsequent performance evaluations and decisions are made but in the analysis we need to bear in mind the factors that may influence the results.

Objective

The objective of the Illinois Agility Run Test is to monitor the development of the athlete's agility.

Required resources

To undertake this test you will require:

— flat surface - a 400 metre Track

— 8 cones

— Stop watch

— Assistant

The Illinois course

The length of the course is 10 metres and the width is 5 metres. On an athletics track, you could use 5 lanes. 4 cones can be used to mark the start, finish and the two turning points. Each cone in the centre is spaced 3.3 metres apart.

How to conduct the test

The Illinois Agility Run Test is conducted as follows:

— The athlete lies face down on the floor at the start point
— On the assistant's command the athlete jumps to his/her feet and negotiates the course around the cones to the finish
— The assistant records the total time taken from their command to the athlete completing the course.

Analysis

Analysis of the result is by comparing it with the results of previous tests. It is expected that, with appropriate training between each test, the analysis would indicate an improvement.

Target group

This test is suitable for team sports but not for individuals where the test would be contraindicated.

Reliability

Reliability would depend upon how strict the test is conducted and the individual's level of motivation to perform the test.

Lateral Change of Direction Test

Testing and measurement are the means of collecting information upon which subsequent performance evaluations and decisions are made but in the analysis we need to bear in mind the factors that may influence the results.

Objective

To monitor the development of the athlete's speed with directional change.

Required resources

To undertake this test you will require

— Flat surface - track

— Three cones

— Stop watch

— Assistant.

How to conduct the test

The three cones are set five metres apart on a straight line.

— The athlete starts at the middle cone

— The Coach gives the signal to start and points in a specific direction, right or left

— The athlete moves to and touches the first cone, returns past the middle cone (start) to the far cone and touches that one and then returns to the middle cone, touching that one.

The coach starts the stopwatch on giving the 'Go' command and stops the watch when the athlete touches the middle cone. The better of the two trails in each starting direction, right and left, are recorded and the best score in each direction is used for scoring.

Analysis

Analysis of the result is by comparing it with the results of previous tests. It is expected that, with appropriate training between each test, the analysis would indicate an improvement.

Target group

This test is suitable for active athletes but not for individuals where the test would be contraindicated.

Reliability

Reliability would depend upon how strict the test is conducted and the individual's level of motivation to perform the test.

Quick Feet Test

Testing and measurement are the means of collecting information upon which subsequent performance evaluations and decisions are made but in the analysis we need to bear in mind the factors that may influence the results.

Objective

The quick feet test provides information on the presence of fast-twitch muscle fibre in the muscles involved in sprinting and indicates your potential to execute quick movements. Hereditary factors such as limb length, muscle attachments, and proportion of fast-twitch fibres do place a limit on one's maximum potential, but we can improve our speed and quickness with proper training.

Required resources

To undertake this test you will require

— Flat surface

— 20 two-foot long sticks or a 20-rung rope ladder

— Stop watch

— Assistant.

How to conduct the test

Place 20 two-foot long sticks 18 inches apart or a 20-rung stride rope ladder on grass or athletics track. Athletes should pump their arms vigorously in a sprint-arm motion and use very little knee lift while running down the ladder without touching the sticks/rungs.

The coach starts the stopwatch when the athlete's foot first touches the ground between the first and second stick/rung and stops the watch when contact is first made with the ground beyond the last stick/rung. Record the better of two trials.

Analysis

Analysis of the result is by comparing it with the results of previous tests. It is expected that, with appropriate training between each test, the analysis would indicate an improvement in the athlete's foot speed.

Normative Data

Speed through a ladder can indicate much about an athlete's quickness. A time of less than 2.8 seconds for males and 3.4 seconds for females for running the length of a 20 rung ladder, one foot in each rung at a time, is considered as excellent for college athletes.

Males	*Time*	*Females*	*Time*
Jnr High School	< 3.8 seconds	Jnr High School	< 4.2 seconds
Snr High School	< 3.3 seconds	Snr High School	< 3.8 seconds
College	< 2.8 seconds	College	< 3.4 seconds

Target group

This test is suitable for active athletes but not for individuals where the test would be contraindicated.

Reliability

Reliability would depend upon, how strict the test is conducted and the individual's level of motivation to perform the test.

SHUTTLE RUN TEST

Testing and measurement are the means of collecting

information upon which subsequent performance evaluations and decisions are made but in the analysis we need to bear in mind the factors that may influence the results.

Objective

The objective of this test is to assess the athlete's ability to accelerate between marked lines and to rapidly change direction.

Required Resources

To undertake this test you will require:

- Two marked parallel lines 9.14m (30 feet) apart
- Two wooden blocks 5 cm x 5 cm x 10 cm
- Stopwatch
- Assistant.

How to conduct the test

- The athlete is required to sprint from the starting line to pick up a block and then place it on the ground behind the starting line. The athlete then sprints to pick up the second block and turns to sprint over the starting line
- The stopwatch is started on the command "Go" and stopped when the athlete's chest crosses the line
- An attempt is not counted if the block is dropped rather than placed on the floor. Also the block must be placed behind and not on the line
- Repeat the test 3 times
- Record the best time.

Analysis

Analysis of the result is by comparing it with the results

of previous tests. It is expected that, with appropriate training between each test, the analysis would indicate an improvement.

Target hroup

This test is suitable for active athletes but not for individuals where the test would be contraindicated.

Reliability

Reliability would depend upon, how strict the test is conducted and the individual's level of motivation to perform the test.

'T' DRILL TEST

Testing and measurement are the means of collecting information upon which subsequent performance evaluations and decisions are made but in the analysis we need to bear in mind the factors that may influence the results.

Objective

To monitor the development of the athlete's speed with directional change.

Required Resources

To undertake this test you will require:

- — Flat surface
- — Four cones
- — A stop watch
- — An assistant.

How to conduct the test

Three cones are set five metres apart on a straight line. A

fourth cone is placed 10 metres from the middle cone so that the cones form a 'T'.

— The athlete starts at the cone at the base of the 'T'
— The coach gives the signal to 'Go' and starts the stop watch
— The athlete runs to the middle cone, touches the cone
— The athlete then side steps 5 metres to the left cone, touches that cone
— The athlete then side steps 10 metres to the far cone and touches that one
— The athlete the side steps 5 metres back to the middle cone, touching that one
— The athlete then runs 10 metres backwards to the base of the 'T' and touches that cone
— The coach stops the watch.

Analysis

Analysis of the result is by comparing it with the results of previous tests. It is expected that, with appropriate training between each test, the analysis would indicate an improvement in the athlete's speed.

Target group

This test is suitable for active athletes but not for individuals where the test would be contraindicated.

Reliability

Reliability would depend upon, how strict the test is conducted and the individual's level of motivation to perform the test.

Zig-Zag Test

Testing and measurement are the means of collecting

information upon which subsequent performance evaluations and decisions are made but in the analysis we need to bear in mind the factors that may influence the results.

Objective

The objective of this test is to monitor the development of the athlete's speed and agility.

Required Resources

To undertake this test you will require:

— 5 cones

— Non slip surface

— Stop watch

— An assistant

How to conduct the test

— Mark out the course with four cones placed on the corners of a rectangle 10 by 16 feet, with one more cone placed in the centre

— The athlete follows the grey route identified on the diagram

— The athlete completes one circuit of the course starting and finishing at the Start and Finish cone (see diagram)

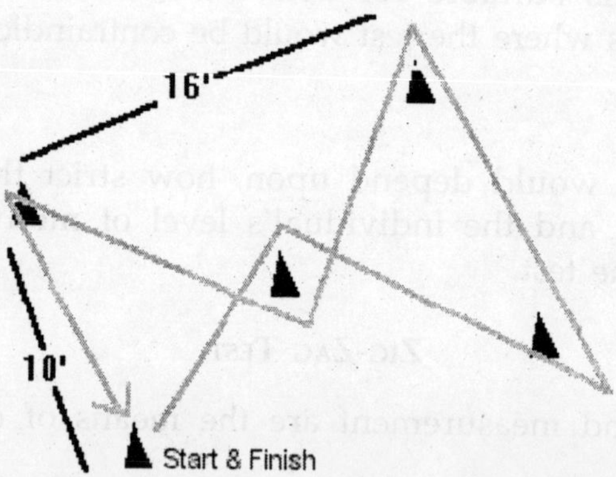

— The assistant records the time to the nearest 0.5 seconds.

Analysis

Analysis of the result is by comparing it with the results of previous tests. It is expected that, with appropriate training between each test, the analysis would indicate an improvement.

Target group

This test is suitable for active athletes but not for individuals where the test would be contraindicated.

Reliability

Reliability would depend upon, how strict the test is conducted and the individual's level of motivation to perform the test.

HIP FLEXION TEST

Testing and measurement are the means of collecting information upon which subsequent performance evaluations and decisions are made but in the analysis we need to bear in mind the factors that may influence the results.

Objective

The objective of this test is to monitor the development of the athlete's hip flexors (the muscles that lift your knees).

Required Resources

To undertake this test you will require:

— Non slip surface.

How to conduct the test

— The athlete lies on their back

— The athlete lifts the left knee and using their hands pulls the left knee to their chest
— Normal flexibility is indicated when their right leg remains flat on the floor
— Hip flexors are considered tight if, as they attempt to lift their left knee toward their chest, their right leg leaves the floor
— Repeat with your other leg.

Analysis

Analysis of the result is by comparing it with the results of previous tests. It is expected that, with appropriate training between each test, the analysis would indicate an improvement.

Target group

This test is suitable for active athletes but not for individuals where the test would be contraindicated.

Reliability

Reliability would depend upon how strict the test is conducted and the individual's level of motivation to perform the test.

Modified Sit and Reach Test

Testing and measurement are the means of collecting information upon which subsequent performance evaluations and decisions are made but in the analysis we need to bear in mind the factors that may influence the results.

Objective

The objective of this test is to monitor the development of the athlete's hip and trunk flexibility.

Required Resources

To undertake this test you will require:

— A 'sit and reach table'

— Yard stick

— An assistant.

How to conduct the test

Starting position

— Sit on the floor with the back and head against a wall, legs fully extended with the bottom of the feet against the sit-and-reach box

— Place the hands on top of each other, stretching the arms forward while keeping the head and back against the wall

— Measure the distance from the fingertips to the box edge with a ruler. This becomes zero or starting point.

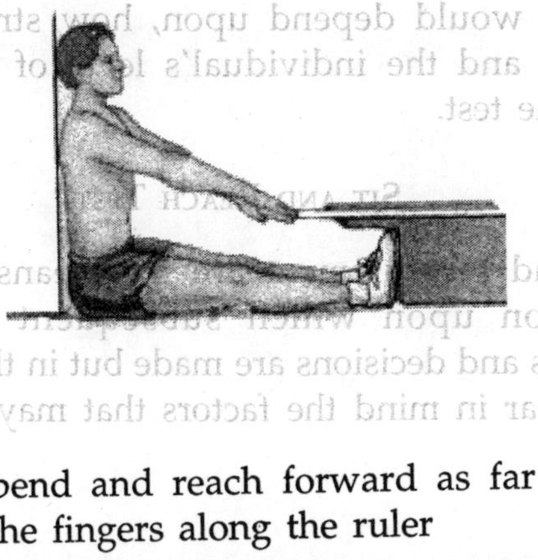

Movement

— Slowly bend and reach forward as far as possible sliding the fingers along the ruler

— Hold the final position for two seconds

— Record the distance reached to the nearest 1/10 of an inch

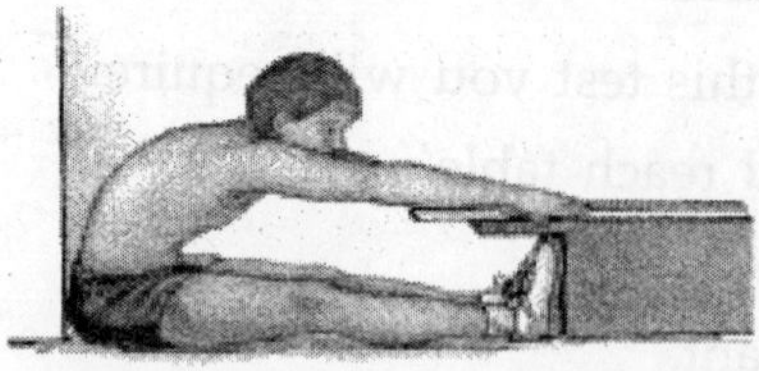

Repeat the test 3 times and note the best distance.

Analysis

Analysis of the result is by comparing it with the results of previous tests. It is expected that, with appropriate training between each test, the analysis would indicate an improvement.

Target group

This test is suitable for active individuals but not for those where the test would be contraindicated.

Reliability

Reliability would depend upon, how strict the test is conducted and the individual's level of motivation to perform the test.

Sit and Reach Test

Testing and measurement are the means of collecting information upon which subsequent performance evaluations and decisions are made but in the analysis we need to bear in mind the factors that may influence the results.

Objective

The objective of this test is to monitor the development of the athlete's lower back and hamstring flexibility.

Required Resources

To undertake this test you will require:

— A 'sit and reach table' or a bench with a ruler
— An assistant.

How to conduct the test

The Sit and Reach Test is conducted as follows:

— The starting position is sitting on the floor with shoes removed, feet flat against the table, and legs straight
— Reach forward and push the fingers along the table as far as possible
— The distance from the finger tips to the edge of the table represents the score for that person
— As the 'sit and reach' table has an overhang of 15 cm, a person who reaches 10 cm past their toes scores 25 cm
— It is important to have several warm-up attempts first, and to record the best score.

Analysis

Analysis of the result is by comparing it with the results of previous tests. It is expected that, with appropriate training between each test, the analysis would indicate an improvement.

Target group

This test is suitable for active individuals but not for those where the test would be contraindicated.

Reliability

Reliability would depend upon, how strict the test is conducted and the individual's level of motivation to perform the test.

Ruler Drop Test

Testing and measurement are the means of collecting information upon which subsequent performance evaluations and decisions are made but in the analysis we need to bear in mind the factors that may influence the results.

Objective

The objective of this test is to monitor the athlete's reaction time.

Required resources

To undertake this test you will require:

— A one 1 metre ruler

— An assistant

How to conduct the test

The ruler is held by the assistant between the outstretched index finger and thumb of the athlete's dominant hand, so that the top of the athlete's thumb is level with the zero centimetre line on the ruler. The assistant instructs the athlete to catch the ruler as soon as possible after it has been released.

The assistant is to record distance between the bottom of the ruler and the top of the athlete's thumb where the ruler has been caught.

Analysis

The algorithm to calculate the reaction speed is $d = vt + \frac{1}{2}at^2$ where

— d = distance in metres

— v = initial velocity = 0

— a = acceleration due to gravity = $9.81 m/s^2$

— t = time in seconds

We need to manipulate $d = vt + ½at^2$ to give us an algorithm for t

As $v = 0$ then $vt = 0$ therefore the algorithm is t = Sqrt(2d/a).

Example

— d = 9cm

— t = sqrt(2 × 0.09 ÷ 9.81)

— t = sqrt(0.01835)

— t = 0.135 seconds

Analysis of the result is by comparing it with the results of previous tests. It is expected that, with appropriate training between each test, the analysis would indicate an improvement.

Core Muscle Strength and Stability Test

Testing and measurement are the means of collecting information upon which subsequent performance evaluations and decisions are made but in the analysis we need to bear in mind the factors that may influence the results.

Objective

The objective of the Core Muscle Strength and Stability Test is to monitor the development of the athlete's abdominal and lower back muscles.

Required Resources

To undertake this test you will require :

— Flat surface

— Mat

— Watch.

How to conduct the test

The Core Muscle Strength and Stability Test is conducted as follows:

— Position the watch on the ground where you can easily see it

— Assume the basic press up position (elbows on the ground) - as in the picture above

— Hold this position for 60 seconds

— Lift your right arm off the ground

— Hold this position for 15 seconds

— Return your right arm to the ground and lift the left arm off the ground

— Hold this position for 15 seconds

— Return your left arm to the ground and lift the right leg off the ground

— Hold this position for 15 seconds

— Return your right leg to the ground and lift the left leg off the ground

— Hold this position for 15 seconds

— Lift your left leg and right arm off the ground

— Hold this position for 15 seconds

— Return you left leg and right arm to the ground

— Lift your right leg and left arm off the ground

— Hold this position for 15 seconds

— Return to the basic press up position (elbows on the ground) - as in the picture above
— Hold this position for 30 seconds.

Analysis

Analysis of the result is by comparing it with the results of previous tests. It is expected that, with appropriate training between each test, the analysis would indicate an improvement.

If you were able to complete this test then it indicates you have good core strength. If you are unable to complete the test then repeat the routine 3 or 4 times a week until you can.

If core strength is poor then the torso will move unnecessarily during motion and waste energy. Good core strength indicates that the athlete can move with high efficiency.

Standing Long Jump Test

Testing and measurement are the means of collecting information upon which subsequent performance evaluations and decisions are made but in the analysis we need to bear in mind the factors that may influence the results.

Objective

To monitor the development of the athlete's elastic leg strength.

Required Resources

To undertake this test you will require:

— Long Jump pit
— 30 metre tape measure
— An assistant

How to conduct the test

The athlete places their feet over the edge of the sandpit. The athlete crouches, leans forward, swings their arms backwards, the jumps horizontally as far as possible, jumping with both feet into the sandpit. The coach should measure from the edge of the sandpit to the nearest point of contact. The start of the jump must be from a static position.

Analysis

Analysis of the result is by comparing it with the results of previous tests. It is expected that, with appropriate training between each test, the analysis would indicate an improvement.

SPRINT BOUND INDEX TEST

Testing and measurement are the means of collecting information upon which subsequent performance evaluations and decisions are made but in the analysis we need to bear in mind the factors that may influence the results.

Objective

To monitor the development of the athlete's elastic leg strength.

Required Resources

To undertake this test you will require:

— 400 metre track - 30 metre marked section on the straight
— Cones
— Stop Watch
— Two assistants.

How to conduct the test

— Begin with one foot on the start line and place the other foot two to three feet behind you.

— Place both of your helpers at the finish line - one to count the number of foot contacts and the other to time your sprint-bound effort over the 30 metre distance.

— On your own command, sprint-bound down the track for the entire 30 metre distance.

— The timer should start the watch when the foot on the start line breaks contact with the ground and then stop the watch when your torso crosses the finish line

— The time is recorded by rounding up to the nearest tenth of a second

— Your second helper is responsible for counting the number of bounds it takes you to reach the finish line.

— The number of bounds should be rounded down to the nearest half-bound.

— Perform three trials, with three to five minutes between each trial.

— Record the results of all three trials.

Calculate the 'sprint-bounding index' for each trial using the following formula:

— Sprint-bound index (SBI) = (no. of bounds) × (time for 30 metres).

Analysis

Analysis of the result is by comparing it with the results of previous tests. It is expected that, with appropriate training between each test, the analysis would indicate an improvement.

Sergeant Jump Test

Testing and measurement are the means of collecting information upon which subsequent performance evaluations and decisions are made but in the analysis we need to bear in mind the factors that may influence the results.

Objective

To monitor the development of the athlete's elastic leg strength.

Required Resources

To undertake this test you will require:

— A wall
— 1 metre Tape Measure
— Chalk
— An assistant.

How to conduct the test

The athlete:

— chalks the end of his finger tips
— stands side onto the wall, keeping both feet remaining on the ground, reaches up as high as possible with one hand and marks the wall with the tips of the fingers (M1)
— from a static position jumps as high as possible and marks the wall with the chalk on his finger tips (M2) The coach then measures the distance from M1 to M2. The test can be performed as many times as the athlete wishes.

Bibliography

Alexeev, V., "Method Of Training", *vol 1 International Weightlifting Journal*, Sofia, Bulgaria 15-19, 1979.

Brynteson, P., & Sinning, W., "The Effects Of Training Frequencies On The Retention Of Cardiovascular Fitness", *Medicine and Science in Sports*, 5, 29-33, 1973.

Christensen, E.H., & Hansen, O., "Working Capacity And Diet", *Scandinavian Archieves of Physiology*, 81, 160-172, 1939.

Cureton, T.K., "The Physiological Effects Of Exercise Programs Upon Adults", Springfield, IL: Thomas, 1969.

DeLorme, T., & Watkins, A. "Progressive Resistance Exercise", New York: Appleton-Century Crofts, 1951.

Gordon, E.E. "Anatomical And Biomechanical Adaptations Of Muscle To Different Exercises", *Journal of the American Medical Association*, 201, 755-758, 1967.

Ikai, M., "Training Of Muscle Strength And Power In Athletes", *Paper presented at F.I.M.S. Congress*, Oxford, England, 1970.

Jackson, J., Sharkey, B.J., & Johnston, L.P., "Cardiorespiratory Adaptations To Training At Specified Frequencies", *Research Quarterly*, 39, 295-300, 1968.

Jackson, C., & Dickinson, A., "Adaptations Of Skeletal Muscle To Strength Or Endurance Training", In W. Grana, J. Lombardo, B. Sharkey, & J. Stone (Eds.), *Advances in Sports Medicine and Fitness* 45-59 Chicago: Year Book Medical, 1988.

Jackson, A.S., & Pollock, M.L., Golding, L.A., Myers, C.R., Sinning, W.E., "The Y's Way To Physical Fitness", *Champaign*, IL: Human Kenetics, 1989.

Kanehisa, H., & Miyashita, M., "Specificity Of Velocity In Strength Training", *European Journal of Applied Physiology* 52, 104-110, 1983.

Kline, G.M., Porcari, J.P., Huntermeister, R., Freedson, P.S., Ward, A., McCarron, R.F., Ross, J., Rippe, J.M., "Estimation Of VO2max From A One Mile Track Walk, Gender, Age, And Body Weight", *Medicine and Science in Sports and Exercise* vol 19 253-259, 1987.

Komi, P., & Buskirk, E.R., "Effects Of Eccentric And Concentric Muscle Conditioning On Tension And Electrical Activity Of Human Muscle", *Ergonomics* 15, 417-422, 1972.

Komi, P. "The Stretch-Shortening Cycle In Human Power Output", In N.C. Jones, N. McCartney, & A.J. McComas (Eds.), *Human Muscle Power*. Champaign, IL: Human Kenetics, 1986.

Lohman, T.G., Roche, A.F., Martorell, R. (Eds.), "Anthropometric Standardization Reference Manual", *Champaign*, IL: Human Kenetics 45-50 51-53 58-63 67-68, 1991.

Massey, B.H., Nelson, R.C., Sharkey, B.J., & Comden, T. "Effects Of High Frequency Electrical Stimulation On The Size And Strength Of Skeletal Muscle", *Journal of Sports Medicine* 5, 136-144, 1965.

Starr, B., "The Strongest Shall Survive", Annapolis, MD: *Fitness Products*, Ldt. 27-37, 1976.

Wilmore, J.H., *Athletic Training And Physical Fitness*, Boston : Allyn & Bacon, 1983.

Index

Adenosine Triphosphate and Phosphate (ATP) 96
Aerobic maintenance sessions 235
Agility Test 272
Anaerobic Lactate (Glycolytic) System 143
Astrand Treadmill Test 263

Balke Treadmill Test 266

Calculation Parameters 60
Cardiovascular Endurance 3
Central nervous system 59
Circuit Training 80
Complex training programs 65
Complex Training 64
Conditioning 62
Core Muscle Strength and Stability Test 289
Creatine Phosphate (CP) 58

Double periodisation 234
Dumbbell Exercises 87
Dynamic flexibility 136

Elastic strength 52
Electromyographic (EMG) 55

Faulkner Test 268

General Endurance 138
Genetic predisposition 56
Goal setting 15
Gymnasiums 11

Hexagonal Obstacle Test 273
Hill running 94
Hip Flexion Test 283

Illinois Agility Run Test 274
Individualisation 238
Interval training 128

Lactic Acid (LA) 58
Lateral Change of Direction Test 275

Marathon circuit 86
Marathon performance 245
Modified Sit and Reach Test 284
Muscle Fibre Hypertrophy 53
Muscle mechanism 74
Muscular strength 21
Musculoskeletal System 144

Neuroendocrine System 144
Neuromuscular pathways 59

Olympic lifts 56

Organised training 129

Personal Best (PB's) 9
Planning preparation 13
Plyometrics 74
Proprioceptive System 144

Repetition Maximum (RM) 56
Reversibility 142
Ruler Drop Test 288
Running-based Anaerobic Sprint Test (RAST) 269

Seated hamstring stretch 26
Sergeant Jump Test 294
Shuttle Run Test 278
Sit and Reach Test 286
Sprint Bound Index Test 292
Standing Long Jump Test 291
Stimulus Magnitude 236
Strength endurance 52
Strength training program 57
Submaximal Tests 261

Team-based sports 131
Three Repetition Maximum (3RM) 56
Training Phases 25
Training Plan 8
Training programme 23

Uick Feet Test 277

Weight training 11
Weight Training 53
Wingate ANaerobic 30 cycle Test (WANT) 269

ZigZag running 2
Zig-Zag Test 281